Playful Perception

Choosing How to Experience Your World

Herbert L. Leff, Ph.D.

Waterfront Books, Inc.
Burlington, Vermont

Cover and interior photos by Herbert Leff
Cover and interior design by David Robinson
Composition by Vanguard Type & Design
Printed in the United States by R.R. Donnelley, Inc.

Library of Congress Cataloging in Publication Data

Leff, Herbert L., 1944
  Playful perception
    1. Creative ability—Problems, exercises, etc.
    2. Perception—Problems, exercises, etc.
    3. Self-actualization (psychology)—Problems, exercises, etc.
BF408.L44   1944   153.7   83-19876
ISBN 0-914525-01-8 (cl)
ISBN 0-914525-00-X (pbk)

PREFACE

The ideas and suggestions in this book represent the fruits of over a decade of research and teaching in the area of perceptual creativity. My main theme is that *we all can create far more interesting, beneficial experiences in everyday life than most of us normally do.* To choose consciously and imaginatively how you are going to experience things is an energizing and enjoyable approach to life. The enhanced creativity and self-direction evidenced by students and research participants I have worked with over the years have amply borne this out. It has been especially gratifying to see people surprise themselves with their ability to create interesting, empowering experiences whenever they want.

Because my purpose here is mainly to share a sampling of procedures that anyone can use to stimulate perceptual creativity and enjoyment, this book is written simply and nontechnically.* You will find several dozen awareness plans and creativity aids for achieving a variety of goals. These goals range from increased fun and aesthetic appreciation to heightened inventiveness and ability to think creatively and cooperatively with other people. Exploring the ideas in these pages should also inspire you to come up with your own special ways and purposes for perceiving playfully. Throughout, the underlying message is that at every moment of your life you have the power to consciously create and enrich your experience of the world.

---

* An account of underlying theory and research can be found in my book *Experience, Environment, and Human Potentials* (New York: Oxford University Press).

Acknowledgments

All our thought is so intertwined with that of other people that I find it difficult to single out just a few thinkers to thank. One especially inspiring book for me, though, has been the now classic *Plans and the Structure of Behavior* by George Miller, Eugene Galanter, and Karl Pribram. I can also trace *Playful Perception*'s underlying themes and commitments back to my student work with John Thibaut of the University of North Carolina and Roger Brown of Harvard University, two psychologists who were not only excellent mentors but very affable human beings as well. More recently, I feel special gratitude to such purveyors of synergy and basic enlightenment as Richard Alpert/Ram Dass, Chris Argyris, Gregory Bateson, Werner Erhard, Marilyn Ferguson, Abraham Maslow, Luke Rhinehart, and Alan Watts. These are but a few of the holistic, humanistic, and transpersonal thinkers who have been helping to expand our culture's consciousness during the past couple of decades.

And then there are my students! There have been hundreds who have taken my environmental psychology and creativity courses while *Playful Perception* was coming to life, and they are here in this book. I regret that it is impossible to specifically acknowledge all their examples and ideas that over time have become woven into my thinking and writing. I hope it will suffice to point out that I have gained much insight and inspiration from my students and that this book in a deep sense has been a cooperative endeavor with them.

Finally, let me acknowledge and thank my family and friends. Among the latter, I feel fortunate to include the publishers, Sherrill and Richard Musty of Waterfront Books. They are actually launching their innovative new company with this book, and they're doing it with a panache, cooperative spirit, and commitment to high quality that would delight any author. Our book designer, David Robinson, also deserves special thanks for his imaginative, careful work. That goes for my secretary, Hildegarde Bolsterle, too, who must know this book as well as anyone after typing so many drafts and revisions over the past few years. But most of all, I want to thank my wife, Ellen, and my son, Jacob, for their support and contributions. This book is affectionately dedicated to them.

To Ellen and Jacob

CONTENTS

INTRODUCTION: **Perceiving with Imagination**   1

SECTION I: **Fun and Flexibility**   11

SECTION II: **Aesthetic Awareness**   29

SECTION III: **Tuning In**   51

SECTION IV: **Evaluating**   67

SECTION V: **Imagining Improvements**   79

SECTION VI: **Basic Enlightenment**   101

SECTION VII: **Synergistic Consciousness**   117

SECTION VIII: **Inventing Your Own**   133

OVERVIEW: **Summary List of Awareness Plans & Creativity Aids**   157

An Invitation

About the Author

PERCEIVING
WITH IMAGINATION

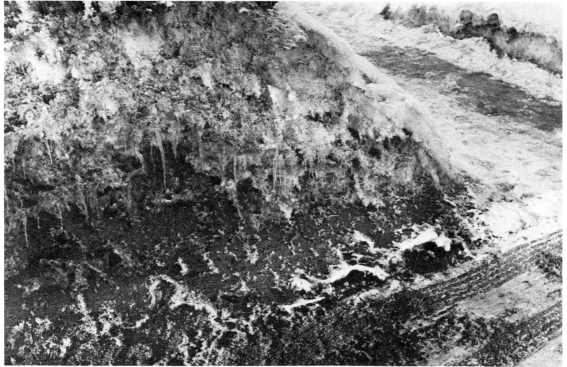

2

Grimy mounds of snow, sprinkled here and there with dog poop, used to become pretty irritating to me as I trekked between home and office in the Vermont winter. Then I devised the simple trick of seeing these surroundings as if I were viewing some weird, otherworldly terrain from an airplane or low-flying spacecraft. The mounds of grimy ice and snow now became strange mountains with intriguing ridges and gorges that I imagined would be exciting to climb. Even the dog poop became some unknown geological formation or perhaps alien architecture. And the trek became fun.

• A participant in one of my research projects reported the following experience when asked to think about how the buildings and landscapes on a particular city block related to nature:

"Thought of all the natural laws that applied to manmade things—all the laws of physics that applied to the fact that the buildings are standing—the basic Buddhist law of impermanence and how all was also decaying—then the natural progression of man which evolved to incorporate sciences and higher learning which created all these buildings and the hospital—saw the scene in the sense that all that happens and is, is nature."

• What would happen if we listened to our children's upsets with the intention of grasping the child's own feelings and view of the situation? Thomas Gordon, in his books on "Parent Effectiveness Training," persuasively argues that this way of listening to children can help them deal with their problems and can contribute to a happier family life for both children and parents.

These are a few examples of perceptual creativity—experiencing the world in imaginative, enriching ways. This book provides you with specific suggestions for a wide variety of such creative ways to perceive the things, people, and events you encounter in everyday life. The main purpose is to help you develop increased mental playfulness and choice in how you experience your world. By the end of the book you will see that we all can gain considerably more enjoyment and insight from our perceptual experience than we often do. We can achieve this by consciously and creatively directing our attention and our thinking about what is around us.

Notice that no matter what situation you are in, you always have some choice among different things to focus your attention on and among different ways to interpret or think about whatever you focus on. When I was walking to and from my office, I could have focused on my own feet or on the buildings around me as well as on the dirty snow. Or I could have distracted myself with thoughts of balmy beaches. And I could have thought of the snow as frozen water or as a memory of winter storms rather than as alien mountains. Although not arbitrary—it's risky not to pay attention to what's underfoot on those icy sidewalks!—my decision to pretend I was zipping along in a low-flying spacecraft was but one of many possibilities open to me.

Each possible way to experience our surroundings can be thought of as an *awareness plan*—a procedure for perceiving and thinking about the world around us. Since this concept is a subtle psychological notion, it may help to draw an analogy from everyday life. You can regard an awareness plan as a kind of mental recipe, in many ways like a recipe for preparing food. A cooking recipe calls for you to select certain food items and to perform certain operations on them—such as, "Get two eggs, crack them open, and separate the whites and yolks." Similarly, an awareness plan calls for you to select certain items and perform certain operations on them. Instead of physically selecting items, like picking up eggs from the supermarket or refrigerator, you mentally select items by focusing your attention on them. (You can even think of the world around you as corresponding to the supermarket and your memory as corresponding to the refrigerator.) Then, instead of performing physical operations (like cracking and separating) as you do with a cooking recipe, when using an awareness plan you perform mental operations like imagining something is upside down, or judging how much you like it, or thinking about new ways to use it.

As you realize, there is far more around you than you can possibly be aware of at any given moment. Hence, you are constantly selecting what to be aware of, although you probably don't make this selection consciously most of the time. Typically, we select what to notice according to fairly automatic awareness plans determined by whatever our immediate goals or activities are. When driving in heavy traffic, for instance, your awareness plan likely is to pay close attention to the cars and traffic signals around you and to plan driving maneuvers to move you toward your destination swiftly and safely. In situations less pressing than this, your awareness plans may seem to arise almost randomly.

What specific ways of perceiving and thinking do you find yourself using when you visit a museum, zoo, aquarium, or other place where things are on exhibit? Could you describe some of these awareness plans fully enough so that another person could learn to look at exhibits the same way you do?

What, for instance, do you find yourself noticing and thinking about when out on a stroll in the evening? If you'll take a few minutes every now and then to watch your mind at work, to notice just what you have been perceiving and thinking about, you'll get an idea of how varied and how automatic your awareness plans usually are.

My research has indicated that we typically view our everyday surroundings with such awareness plans as the following:

> briefly noticing and classifying the things around us;
> thinking of personally meaningful associations to these things;
> evaluating what we notice;
> formulating questions about items or events noticed;
> thinking about personal goals or tasks.

Of course, the full array of "normal" awareness plans is actually limitless, and it is clear that each of us shifts awareness plans as a result of changes in mood, situation, role, goal, and any number of other influences on the way we think and perceive. However, common observation as well as my research indicates that most of us do not typically make conscious choices about which awareness plans to use.

This book encourages you to make such conscious choices! Experimenting with its suggestions can help you break out of old perceptual ruts and explore new awareness plans that can enliven your experience. Just as developing skill in using good new recipes can add zest to your cooking and nutrition, so expanding your repertoire of useful awareness plans can improve the flavor and value of your inner experiences. For instance, practicing with certain plans, such as thinking of everything as alive or as a work of art, can lead you to increased fun and aesthetic enjoyment in perceiving your everyday surroundings. Other awareness plans can help you gain increased insight and interest concerning the social and physical environment. Still others can lead you to raise your creativity in detecting and solving problems, and some can even facilitate constructive shifts in dealing with other people. In the course of this book, each of these areas of potential gain will be explored.

The most important gain, though, will be that you will increase your choice about the quality of your experience. Awareness plans provide our most promising path to exercise such direct choice. Have you ever tried, say, to change one of your beliefs or emotions or values by simply choosing to change it? Our minds generally won't cooperate in such matters! It is very hard for most of us to will a change in a belief, feeling, or value without any intermediate steps. But it's a snap, by comparison, to choose to change the focus of your attention or to choose to think about something in a new way. This ability to shift awareness plans at will gives us the key to conscious self-direction of the quality of our ongoing experience. Even though we may not be able to directly control our emotions or beliefs, we can readily influence our feelings and our views of the world by creating and choosing appropriate awareness plans.

What Lies Ahead

Your journey through this book will introduce you to dozens of special awareness plans and creativity aids. All told, this collection of suggestions on how to use your powers of attention and imagination offers doorways to expanded awareness on a variety of fronts. The early plans are intended mainly for fun, fantasy, and appreciation. These are followed by awareness plans designed to stimulate your insight and curiosity about your surroundings. All of this paves the way for a section on imagining beneficial changes in the world around you. Beyond this you'll come to some suggestions for treating everything in life in a constructive, "enlightened" fashion and for relating to other people in creatively cooperative ways. Finally, you'll be encouraged to invent new awareness plans on your own, with the help of some creativity aids fitted to that purpose.

The eight sections of the book flow in a progression from focus on your own immediate experience to increasing concentration on creative problem-solving and cooperative relations with other people. The overall movement is also from fanciful to "realistic" modes of perceiving and thinking. The early awareness plans will quickly give you a sense of how easily you can consciously shape your perceptual experience in interesting new ways. The resulting mental flexibility will also come in handy for the later focus on creative problem-solving. In addition, you should find that experimenting with all these awareness plans will help you to more easily understand other people's points of view and to develop skill in cooperative social relations.

To make your journey as interesting and involving as possible, the major awareness plans are presented as instructions or questions for viewing an accompanying photograph. You will likely gain most from reading this book if you proceed at a leisurely pace and *thoroughly explore* each awareness plan and creativity aid as you come to it. I have some additional advice coming up momentarily, but first here is a preview of the whole book:

Section I. Fun and Flexibility—A sampling of awareness plans that lead you to whimsical, imaginative ways of experiencing the world and that impart fun and flexibility to your perceiving.

Section II. Aesthetic Awareness—Several plans to help you find more beauty in everyday objects and places, and to sharpen your aesthetic sensitivity generally.

Section III. Tuning In—Awareness plans to help you become more insightful about your surroundings, stimulate your curiosity, and activate your knowledge about what you perceive.

Section IV. Evaluating—A few plans to stimulate your insight about alternative ways to evaluate or judge things around you.

Section V. Imagining Improvements—Three core awareness plans and a dozen creativity aids for thinking up beneficial changes to make around you (and for thinking up ways to achieve those changes).

Section VI. Basic Enlightenment—Five very special awareness plans to inspire you to experience life in a fulfilling way, whatever it brings.

Section VII. Synergistic Consciousness—Some simple, but powerful plans to help you develop holistic thinking and a creatively cooperative orientation toward other people.

Section VIII. Inventing Your Own—Three "meta-plans" and twelve creativity aids for developing your own special ways of perceiving and interpreting the world.

Some Preliminary Advice

Trying out new awareness plans should be *fun*, an adventure. If you are energetic in really "getting into" a new way of perceiving and thinking— even if just for a few minutes—you will find your whole experience of the world changed for that period of time. And in the case of some awareness plans, the change in the way you experience things can be radical (as in my treks through the dirty snow, for instance). Since all of the upcoming plans are intended to help you enrich your experience, you should generally find the changes to your liking. To get the most out of these new experiences, though, do keep the following points in mind.

1. Match plans and goals. For instance, use aesthetic or fanciful awareness plans only when you actually feel like perceiving aesthetically or fancifully. Basically, the first and most important step in using a new awareness plan is to pick it in accordance with an honest appraisal of what kind of experience you want to create. It especially helps to think of specific goals that matter to you—say, reducing anxiety or boredom in some situation, or becoming more effective at work—and then look for ways to use various awareness plans to help you accomplish the goals.

2. Give yourself a chance to practice with a new plan for a while before passing final judgment on its usefulness. Try out different ways of using it, make subtle twists in it to suit your mood and situation, combine it with other awareness plans, and use it in different types of situations. In essence, *explore* its possibilities; experiment with it!

3. Engage other people to explore awareness plans with you. It's not hard. Most people are willing to try playful, aesthetic, interest-arousing, or imaginative ways of experiencing. And discussing different reactions among a group of people focusing on the same scene or event is at least a pleasant diversion. You will likely find that involving other people in trying out new ways of perceiving and thinking will make the whole process more creative and more fun.

4. Keep a personal journal of your experiences with new awareness plans. This will yield some interesting reading to you later on and can give you a basis for judging the relative value of different plans. The journal will also spur you to seriously explore new plans and to think up original ones of your own. Even if you don't start out with a full-fledged journal, I urge you at least to jot down suggestions from this book that you would like to try out and also any new plans that you invent. If you'll carry such a list with you, I think you'll find many occasions—such as tedious waits or boring tasks—when it can provide ready suggestions for interesting ways to use your mind.

5. Start out by consciously observing and choosing the awareness plans you normally use. Bear in mind that any new behavior, including the use of special awareness plans, can seem a little artificial and difficult at first. In addition to the above four suggestions, a good way to alleviate this problem is simply to reflect every now and then on what you have just been attending to and how you have been thinking about it. Once you realize that you are always using *some* awareness plan whether you consciously choose it or not, you'll likely feel less reluctant to deliberately select how you want your mind to operate. Indeed, you may well come to feel that true spontaneity in the use of awareness plans actually lies in consciously choosing them rather than just letting your habitual patterns of perception and thought hold sway.

• To sum up, you will gain most from new awareness plans by using them for goals you genuinely desire at the time, by practicing a new plan until you become skillful at it, by involving other people, by keeping a journal of your experiences and ideas (or at least a reminder list of favorite plans), and by consciously observing and choosing your normal awareness plans. Of course, you need not do all of these things in order to derive benefits from this book. The suggestions are offered simply as advice that will likely help out and that has been effective for the people I have worked with. **The one thing that really is essential if you are to gain what this book has to offer, though, is to actually USE the awareness plans you will be reading about!**

FUN AND FLEXIBILITY

Do you enjoy being imaginative, lighthearted, humorous, and maybe even a little crazy? If so, the awareness plans in this section should suit you just fine, since their purpose is to help you realize how easy it is to view the world in fanciful ways. Do you get bored while waiting for buses or meetings? The plans coming up, and similar ones you yourself devise, could prove very useful at such times. Would you like to spice up casual walks, or add some pizzazz to mowing the lawn or washing the dishes? Well, here are awareness plans to help you get rolling.

As you know, this whole book is meant to be treated with at least a dash of playfulness. But this section is intended for playfulness in the extreme. This one is for loosening up and warming up, for deliberately letting yourself be whimsical, even silly. It's all in your mind, of course; you don't have to *act* silly or do anything that other people might see as peculiar, for goodness sake. All you need to do is suspend your ordinary ways of interpreting your surroundings and temporarily substitute zany new ways of thinking about what you perceive. The rewards range from making mundane experiences more interesting and entertaining to boosting your ability to come up with creative new ideas.

Please bear in mind, as well, that my intention is not to lay out a hard and fast program of *the* awareness plans to use. What I most want to do is stimulate your power to shape your own experience imaginatively. You will benefit most if you not only try out the specific plans found on these pages but also develop variations and entirely new awareness plans of your own.

Seeing Everything Around You as *Alive*

What if all the things in this scene were alive and conscious? What might these creatures be thinking and feeling? What sorts of personalities, cares, and goals do you think they would have? How do you think they would feel about each other, and what would their conversations be about? What would they find humorous or sad? What kinds of questions would you like to ask them, and what do you think they might ask you?

It has intrigued me for years that this particular awareness plan is so popular with participants in my research and courses. Why is it so much fun? Part of the reason may hinge on seeing the world as a more interesting, lively arena—and as a relatively friendly place where you're certainly not alone. (Ever think of your furnace as an oil-guzzling pet, for instance?) Or sometimes seeing things this way can add a little excitement in life, as when you start to guess that all lights or books are visitors (invaders?) from another world! In addition to sheer fun, though, regarding things as alive can be of practical value if guided by a social conscience. For instance, would you like to kindle some enthusiasm for cleaning up litter? If so, thinking of garbage cans as helpless creatures that need to be fed just might do the trick.

Thinking Up
Past and Future *Reincarnations*
for Things Around You

What if everything around us were not only alive but also caught up in cycles of reincarnation, progressing from one life to the next on the basis of its goodness or karma? You might then entertain yourself by guessing plausible past and future "lives" for anything you happen to notice. For instance, how many alternative reincarnations can you think up for a toilet or a roll of bathroom tissue? That toilet over there, say, might have lived out its previous life as an ashtray or a spittoon and be en route to its next life as perhaps a sewage treatment plant (if it has good karma) or a drainpipe for an automatic dishwasher (if it does not). See how long a string of progressively "better" and "worse" lives you can envision for this or some other object you pick.

This awareness plan was suggested by a friend of mine, possessed of an irrepressible and irreverent sense of humor. As with most of the plans in this book, you can use this one on just about anything. Right now, what are some reincarnations you can think up for a particular song, item of household furniture, hobby, organization, occupation, environmental problem? What effect does thinking about things in this way have on your feelings about them?

Dreaming Up *Alternative Meanings* for the Things and Events Around You

See how many different interpretations you can think of for what is going on in this scene. To take some examples, could this be an ad for something? (What?) Part of a movie being filmed? (If so, what are some alternative plots you can think up?) Part of some important news story just breaking? A crime of some sort? A religious ritual perhaps? (What would the religion be like, and what would be the significance of the acts and things shown here?) Part of a psychology experiment? A contest or game of some kind? How about something weird, like a case of time travel? Or could this be part of an art exhibit, or a political campaign? What other meanings can you think up?

I'm sure you get the idea behind this freewheeling awareness plan. Just dream up a variety of alternative interpretations for things and events you notice—and take a few moments to savor each new meaning and its implications for what's "really" going on around you. This is great to try at sporting events, where you might, say, watch a basketball game as a new form of dance, an elaborate religious ceremony, or a humorist's rendering of a committee meeting. Or you might spice up your travels on buses by thinking of billboards or overheard snatches of conversation as coded spy messages, pronouncements of a supreme guru, keys to solving a personal problem, or punchlines to jokes. You can even carry this way of thinking to some philosophical depth by trying out alternative imagined meanings for life or reality. For example, what difference does it make to the way you experience things if you view this life as your only one versus viewing it as but a way station in a progression of reincarnations? Or what happens when you deliberately think of the world we know as but one of many "parallel universes" or levels of reality? From the ridiculous to the sublime, dreaming up alternative meanings is a way to help yourself see the world as a bit richer, livelier, and more mysterious.

Interpreting Things and Events as the *Reverse* of What You Normally Think They Are

Let's take as a simple example seeing the room you are in as if it were in fact upside down right now. That is, imagine that the floor you see really used to be the ceiling and what appears to be the ceiling is supposed to be the floor. (Who knows, this might just give you some off-the-wall ideas for new interior decorating!) Or try mentally reversing the relative values of things around you. Stuff in trash cans, for instance, might be seen as priceless, while cars, money, and skyscrapers would be mere discardable junk. As another example, you can mentally reverse cause/effect relations and see cars as directing drivers, lights shining as causing electricity to flow, hearing the music as causing the record player to operate, and so on. Or you might try reversing your view of what's public property and what's private, or inside/outside (so that trees might then be seen as interior furniture, TV's as outdoor ads, and wind and rain as special air conditioning). There is, of course, no limit to the reversals you can perform with the help of your mind. Good/bad, random/orderly, work/play, give/take—the possibilities are limitless.

The purpose of this nuttiness, incidentally, is to help you add to your mental flexibility, perhaps stimulate some ideas for constructive change, and provide inexpensive entertainment. (Or we might reverse our world view and say that the purpose here is to put us in touch with reality. . . .)

Imagining *New Uses* for Things Around You

How many different uses can you think of for shoes? (At these prices, the more, the better!) Could they be used somehow as toys? What sorts of toys would kids of different ages make of them? How many educational uses can you think up? See if you can figure out some ways to use shoes as musical instruments, as communication devices or aids, and as money-makers of some kind (other than selling them). Can you devise some way to use shoes in connection with a hobby you now enjoy? Overall, what's the silliest new use you can envision for shoes? What's the most practical new use you can come up with?

Directing your awareness to visions of new uses for everyday things can clearly be both enjoyable and, well, useful. Often it's helpful to start your mind on this track by thinking of uses for things that normally do have a lot of different applications. Tape, rubber bands, plastic wrap, or spoons are good examples here. But once you get the feel of inventing multiple uses on the spur of the moment, challenge yourself. Try devising possible uses for things you normally consider useless. Some examples might be broken glass, empty toothpaste tubes, dead leaves, and even bad moods, colds, or embarrassment. One good procedure for this is to imagine that you want to sell the thing and need to point out interesting uses to potential buyers. But there's no need to worry unduly about practicality; a little silliness can spur your creativity and fun.

Viewing the World
as if You Were an *Animal*
(or Even a *Thing*)

How would you perceive this scene if you were a dog? What kinds of things would be important for you to know about the cat and the people who live in the house, for instance? Now switch and imagine that you are another cat coming over to visit. How does this change the way you regard the scene? To get a little wilder, switch again and now think of yourself as a ball of string. What does this do to the way you think of the scene? Or you might go still farther out and imagine that you are heat or the wind. How does this change your view of things and your thoughts? Or what if you imagine yourself to be love, death, beauty, or time?!

———————————

Obviously, this awareness plan can help you shift away from your usual ways of thinking of yourself and your world. Taking on such wild roles can be both entertaining and emotionally enriching. You might expand your empathic abilities and your flexibility in how you think of yourself. You can even extend this role-taking procedure to encompass the whole of your surroundings. If you are in a room, for instance, try imagining that you *are* the room and that all of its contents are part of yourself. Or imagine that you are a whole organization that you belong to, your whole city or town, or even the entire planet. The parts of your organization, city, or planet would then become like cells in your body. Imagine what emotions, sensations, and thoughts you would have, and how you would react to the events going on "inside you."

Some Additional Awareness Plans for Fun and Flexibility

- Viewing all things as edible and trying to figure out how each would taste.

- Imagining that things you notice are really transportation devices and thinking about how each works and how it would feel to travel that way.

- Seeing objects around you as actually the *tops* of structures going deep underground and guessing what these structures are like.

- Regarding each thing you notice as if it were the center or main reason for its surroundings (thus a lawn might be seen as requiring that the house be built so that people would live nearby and water the grass).

- Thinking of everything as artificial (so that insects are tiny, powered machines; people are robots; clouds are movie props; and so on.)

- Seeing everything as randomly thrown together.

- Noticing resemblances for things around you (say, a bus may remind you of a loaf of bread on wheels, or an airplane may sound like a giant swarm of mosquitoes, or everything may suggest some bodily part or other).

- Thinking of poetic imagery to express what you perceive in your surroundings.

- Thinking of how various games would be played in places you encounter (such as hide 'n seek in your office building or baseball in the grocery store).

• Looking for something humorous in everything you notice.

• Regarding inanimate things around you as cooperating or competing with each other.

• Thinking of everything and everyone as "out to get you" (the paranoia awareness plan—be careful if you try this one!).

• Thinking of everyone and everything as really loving you, and regarding everything you encounter as a friendly gift.

• Thinking of time as moving backward, so that everything is actually getting younger or newer as each moment passes.

• Seeing the world as if it is your own painting suddenly come to life (you might then ask yourself why you painted it just this way).

• Regarding whatever you're doing as a game—or figuring out some way to make it into a game.

———————————

○ What new whimsical awareness plans of your own can you add to this list right now?

SECTION II

AESTHETIC AWARENESS

So far you've been exploring techniques to develop a more flexible and imaginative approach to perceiving everyday situations. You should now have a feeling for your inherent power to shift the way you interpret just about anything you encounter. In addition, you have been expanding your ability to entertain yourself just through the way you perceive and think about the things around you. This section carries the theme of enjoying perceptual experience from the realm of fanciful imagination to that of discovering and appreciating beauty in things as they are.

The central message here is that **you can create aesthetic experiences for yourself anytime you choose to do so.** We all know that beauty lies in the beholder's eye, but how many of us follow through on the implication that we can tune ourselves to experience beauty whenever we wish? Everyday sights and sounds that we so commonly overlook—puddles, rusty fences, shadows, the sky, the sound of rain or rustling leaves—can provide us with genuine aesthetic experiences if we stop to perceive them in creatively sensitive ways. This can even be true of telephone poles and crushed cans if we bend our minds to it. Beauty or ugliness, numbness or sensitivity—such choices rest much more within our grasp than we typically realize. The awareness plans now coming up illustrate how you can consciously choose at any moment to perceive the world afresh and with aesthetic delight.

Searching Your Surroundings for Everything That Strikes You as *Beautiful or Aesthetically Interesting*

How much beauty can you find in each of these scenes? Spend a little time carefully studying each scene for anything that catches your fancy as aesthetically appealing or interesting. (You might also return to these two photos after you've explored the other awareness plans in this section.) _____

Looking out for beauty around you is a delightful and sense-opening awareness plan to use just about anytime. Here are a few simple procedures that can help out even in apparently drab environments:

- Try concentrating on each of your senses in turn. Often a locale that leaves a lot to be desired in the way it looks will offer some interesting sounds or smells if you take the time to notice.

- Examine reflections. Reflections are all around us—in puddles and wet pavement, in windows, in fenders and doorhandles, in dishes, even in mirrors. And they are quite a boon, since they often reveal shimmering, glistening, transformed images that appear more beautiful than the things being reflected.

- Concentrate on shadows. This is especially interesting to do with moving shadows, such as your own when you're out for a walk during a sunny day or on a brightly lit street at night. Even when watching a ball game, you can produce an unusual aesthetic experience by focusing on the shifting shadows of the players. (Watch it if you're the sportscaster, though!) And who can deny the beauty of lengthening shadows in late afternoon on a clear day?

- See if you can call up pleasant associations to what you are perceiving. For instance, a snow-covered scene might remind you of a picture postcard or the Christmas season. Or you could focus on arousing pleasant childhood associations to places, objects, people, or events that even vaguely remind you of things you enjoyed as a kid. The key here is simply to look for "beauty by association."

- Team up with another person or two, and take turns pointing out sights, sounds, and whatnot that you think would appeal to each other. See if you can guess what your partner would especially enjoy noticing in your shared surroundings.

Looking for Scenes
in Your Surroundings That
Would Make the *Best Photographs*

Look around wherever you are right now and pretend that you have a camera with only a few frames of film left—and that you want to capture the most interesting, beautiful, or personally meaningful images that you can. Also, this is your only chance to take any of these pictures, so you're very eager to find something worth photographing.

If you've ever toted a real camera around, I'm sure you'll recognize this awareness plan as one you've spontaneously used as you were running out of film. You can really perk up your aesthetic awareness, though, by simply pretending to have a camera. Limiting yourself to a few pictures seems to heighten sensitivity and discrimination, and most people report enjoying this plan most when they imagine their film supply is low. However, it is a good touch to add some "accessories" now and then, such as an imagined zoom or close-up lens, movie camera, or even tape recorder.

Viewing Everyday Things as if They Were *Art Exhibits*

Try regarding this sink full of dishes as if it were an avant-garde exhibit at a renowned art museum. Since you know that all the exhibits here have been chosen for their high aesthetic merit, you might ask yourself questions like the following: What exactly is beautiful or interesting about this sinkfull, especially when carefully examined? What does this work of art communicate—what feelings, moods, thoughts about life or society, what sort of "statement"? Why has this been chosen for public exhibit; why do art critics and museum curators value it so much? What can be learned about good aesthetic design from this exhibit— things like harmony, balance, clever use of materials, beauty in forms and shadings, surprise, expressiveness? You might also think to yourself that much time, energy, and exquisite artistic skill must have gone into this work of art, which, like other art works, was lovingly created to add value to our experience of the world.

Bear in mind that simply putting some otherwise nondescript thing on exhibit in an actual art museum can prompt visitors to find beauty or other aesthetic significance in it. Mangled metal, old furniture, bits of paper—*anything* can turn up in real art exhibits! The basic idea in this awareness plan is to use the way you look at real public art works as a way to look at anything. Pick any common object, such as a telephone pole or a crumpled paper bag, and apply all of those "museum" questions and thoughts to it, imagining that it is actually the work of a great artist. With just a little practice, you should be able to appreciate practically anything in the world as if it were an artistic creation.

Indeed, it is even possible to view your whole environment as if it were a single vast art work replete with planned, but often subtle, aesthetic effects. Then interpret everything around you —sights, sounds, smells, the activities of people, organizations, all of it—as part of this wondrous aesthetic "happening." When you perceive everything this way, the world still appears the same physically; but it seems a lot more beautiful.

Experiencing the World as a Collection of *Abstract Forms*

As you carefully examine the shapes, shadows, textures, and patterns in this photograph of a spiral fire-escape, focus exclusively on pure visual forms without labeling what you see. In short, look at these forms as if they were intended as works of purely *abstract* art, having no meaning or purpose beyond their immediate visual impact. Does this help you experience beauty in the curved and straight lines, the patterns of three-dimensional and flat shapes, the contrasts of light and dark, and the total array of forms?

How many things can you find around you right now that are easy to see as pleasing abstract forms? You might start by focusing on the colors—and especially the fine shadings of color—in whatever catches your eye. (Ignore the names of the colors, but carefully explore and linger on any color patches you find especially appealing.) It also helps to stare at an object for a while; the longer you look, the more you notice and the less you think about labels. Even better is to imagine that you are making a meticulously accurate painting or sculpture of what you are seeing. This really helps you observe closely without mentally verbalizing or evaluating.

Although it may be a little difficult at first to see things as "abstract forms," the rewards of success can be profound. With perseverance, and a little luck, you will be able to discover new beauty and aesthetic interest virtually *anywhere* by the use of this awareness plan. The key is to rest your attention firmly on the colors, shapes, textures, and patterns around you without labeling or interpreting what you see. In a nutshell, *just* see! And you can extend this to your other senses as well. Perceiving sounds, touch sensations, and odors as pure (abstract) sensory experiences can be as aesthetically enriching as abstract seeing. Enjoy!

Finding Special or *Unique* *Value* in Everything You Notice

Although mailboxes may not typically seem like things of beauty, let's see what happens if you concentrate on the unique or special qualities of a mailbox. To help you appreciate a mailbox—or anything else—try asking, "What if this were the only one of its kind?" Just think what a creative invention it would seem: You can write a message to someone anywhere, drop it in this safe, weatherproof metal container any time of the day or night, and know that the message will be picked up and conveyed. Also, note the simplicity and ease of operation of the mailbox, its unobtrusive but convenient placement, its maintenance-free, highly durable design. What other special qualities or values can you think of that a mailbox has? Can you use these to see beauty in the function and meaning of mailboxes—and perhaps even in their squat form?

This awareness plan goes beyond the more purely sensory and artistic focus of the other aesthetic plans, and is intended to help you deepen your appreciation of the functions as well as the appearance of objects. You can also use it to enrich your perception of events, people, organizations, and ideas, in addition to inanimate objects. Just as you might find greater beauty in your bath towel by focusing on its unique qualities of pliability, softness, and ability to dry you off, so you might increase your appreciation of a picnic, a song, an acquaintance, or even yourself by contemplating the special contributions that each makes to life.

Judging the *Degree of Beauty* in Your Surroundings, Using Many Different Criteria

How would you evaluate the aesthetic qualities of each of these scenes? What criteria do you find yourself using? How easy is it for you to find beauty versus ugliness if you set yourself to do each in turn? What happens if you use some of the earlier awareness plans in this section to look at these scenes? Can you think of some different criteria for judging beauty? Perhaps you can try reversing some of your usual standards, so that if you normally like neatness, you could try seeing messiness as a new criterion of beauty. Or you might take on different roles and ask what criteria for beauty each suggests. How, for instance, do you think a nutritionist would evaluate the beauty of these scenes? Or how would a sculptor, a pornographic movie-maker, a fly, or a lightning bolt evaluate the beauty here? Finally, is there anything in either scene that you think people would be unwise to try to see as beautiful?

———————————————

This awareness plan is intended to help you broaden and sharpen your sensitivity to alternative types of aesthetic value. It's also designed to help you reflect both on your surroundings and on the standards you actually use for judging beauty.

Regarding Everything as a Possible *Inspiration* for a New Work of Art

As you look at this picture, pretend that you are a great painter, sculptor, writer, composer, or whatever type of artist fits your mood. What ideas for paintings, sculptures, poems, music, and so on, can you derive from the scene or from particular parts of it? You might look for inspiration in physical forms, feelings or moods you see suggested, or associations and thoughts the scene arouses for you. See how clear an image you can generate for the type of artwork the scene inspires. And remember, you are a *great* artist—so you can be unabashedly enthusiastic about your ideas, whatever they are.

If you make it a point now and then to see the world as if you are a talented artist who gets inspired by everything in sight, you'll be surprised at how much aesthetic value you can find in everyday things. Even things as ordinary as a crack in the sidewalk, a shot in the arm, or a howling puppy might well trip off ideas for a painting, play, dress design, or whatever else is your artist's specialty. As, say, a sculptor, you could go on a walk and see anything and everything—trees, people, traffic signals, clouds—as if they were incipient sculptures, ideas and forms begging to be cast in bronze or represented by strips of aluminum foil. And the more artistic roles you try, the more beauty you're likely to find.

A Playful Aesthetic Activity

Now that you've had a chance to sample a wide range of aesthetically enlivening awareness plans, you might like to try the following activity with some friends (or perhaps your children). Just about everybody I know who's tried it has enjoyed the activity and been surprised at how creative and aesthetically inspired they feel afterward. Here it is:

Preliminary: Collar one to three friends willing to go with you to an art museum and willing to try slightly nutty ways of thinking.

Phase 1: Visit an art museum with these friends. If no museum is handy, a craft shop, a fine gift store, or even a jewelry store can be substituted; but a museum is best. While in the museum (or substitute), spend the first few minutes looking at the exhibits as you normally do. Then see if you can tell each other what sorts of things you tend to notice and how you think about the things on exhibit. That is, describe your normal museum awareness plans to each other. (For instance, you might find yourself noticing mostly sculptures or mostly paintings, wondering about the age of art works or about what feelings the artist wanted to communicate, and so on.) As soon as each of you has described how she or he is looking at the exhibits, *trade* these awareness plans with each other so that you will now try to see the exhibits the way one of your friends does and he or she will try to see the way you do. Spend at least ten or fifteen minutes using each other's awareness plans and talking with each other about what you are noticing.

Phase 2: Go outside and use some of the same awareness plans you used inside the museum to experience things around you. That is, look at the things outside the museum the same way you were looking at exhibits on the inside. Talk with your friends about what each of you is noticing and experiencing. Spend about ten minutes on this phase.

Phase 3: Now the real fun begins. Pretend you are a team of great artists. Each of you can be any type of artist you like—muralist, composer, architect, stager of happenings, moviemaker, skywriter, whatever you wish. But think of yourselves as a team that has always worked together to produce the fabulous art works for which you are all justly renowned. Pretend you currently have a commission to produce, as a team, a magnificent public work of art. Your budget is whatever you need. Although you've only got about a half-hour to plan out your project, with your group's talents this is plenty of time. Your job now: **Use objects and events around you as sources of inspiration for planning this work of art** (and actually plan it out).

Phase 4: Still acting as a group, invent ways of thinking and perceiving that would help people to find more beauty around them. Base these new aesthetic awareness plans on your experiences in Phases 1-3, and think up as many as you can in ten minutes. You can make it a contest to see who can generate the most or the best plans, but your group may be more creative if you just build on each other's ideas. (You might conclude by devising another off-the-wall aesthetic activity for your next get-together!)

A Cautious Send-Off

Once you've become skillful in using the awareness plans in this section, you should indeed be able to create aesthetic experiences anytime you choose. But, you may rightly ask, aren't there some practical and even ethical risks in perceiving normally ugly or unpleasant things as beautiful? If we did this all the time, wouldn't we desensitize ourselves to poverty, environmental problems, and other sources of human suffering? And what if surgeons learned to stand awestruck at the fascinating colors in tumors instead of cutting them out?! Well, that last question may be unfairly extreme, but in fact there are genuine risks in "over-aestheticizing" our experience. Not only is there the danger of stifling our action, but we might also undercut our normal ethical sensitivities. Imagine, for instance, replacing sorrow or agitation with aesthetic pleasure while viewing a grisly automobile wreck or the site of a Nazi concentration camp.

No doubt about it, there are some real dangers lurking amidst the pleasures to be derived from awareness plans to perceive aesthetically. However, the problems are mainly those of *over*indulgence, and with the aid of a little common sense we can avoid the dangers while still reaping the considerable benefits such plans bestow.

First, consider that no source of pleasure is immune to potential problems of overindulgence. Eating, sunbathing, meditating, sex, and even work all help to illustrate the common-sense principle of doing things in moderation and when appropriate. The central idea is not to sacrifice all other values in the service of one single value. Enjoying aesthetic experiences through the use of special awareness plans should surely present no more of a problem than the examples just listed.

Second, the realization of our potentials for an effective, fulfilling life requires skill in using many different ways of thinking and perceiving. Solving problems and making ends meet certainly call for thinking in practical terms—for defining goals and figuring out effective behavior to reach them. But many of life's possible joys hinge also on our capacity to perceive appreciatively and aesthetically. It would thus be a mistake, from the point of view of full human development, to rely exclusively on any single mental approach to the world, whether aesthetic or practical. Developing skill in using a wider and wider range of awareness plans should help us guard against any temptation to narrowness.

Furthermore, perceiving aesthetically can in fact increase our awareness of environmental problems and even help us to be more creative in imagining improvements in our surroundings. For instance, looking at a place or object intensely and with special attention to its immediate sensory qualities can alert you to pollutants and trash you might not otherwise notice. Although some of these, such as oil floating on a puddle or a rusty can in the woods, might have interesting shapes or pleasing colors, just becoming aware of their presence can heighten your concern for environmental quality. Moreover, sensitizing yourself to actual spots of beauty can help you generate ideas for improving any environment you encounter. The more aware you become of the types of things you like, the easier it should be to envision possibilities for improvement.

Finally, you can temper your aesthetic sensitivity with whatever measure of social and environmental consciousness you like. If the well-being of Earth and of other people is important to you, you can choose what to perceive aesthetically in accordance with those values. When at the site of a Nazi concentration camp or even a smog-shrouded slum, use a different type of awareness plan! Or if you do wish to see beauty, you can look for signs of human courage or other things that are consistent with your values. You can even make social or environmental values part of your very definition of what is beautiful for you. Again, the choice of how to experience the world is always available to us. Beauty *is* in the eye of the beholder.

TUNING IN

Up to this point you have been increasing your ability to reinterpret your surroundings in ways that playfully exercise your imagination and that create aesthetic experiences. The goals so far have centered on having more fun and being more appreciative in perceiving the things around you. While the awareness plans in this section are also intended to help you enjoy everyday experiences more, they include the added goal of increasing your insight into what is present around you. More than before, the focus will now be on learning more about your surroundings and integrating your wealth of knowledge about the world into your ongoing experience.

Consider that most of us do know quite a bit about the world, but we often miss chances to use this knowledge to add insight and interest to our perceptions. You might know a lot about cars, for instance, and yet seldom think about what is actually going on inside the automobiles you see. In addition, we overlook or casually observe so many things in our surroundings that would prove fascinating if we took the time to examine them carefully. For a variety of reasons, we can obtain satisfaction simply from becoming aware of previously unnoticed things and from gaining any new insights into our surroundings or ourselves. These reasons include feelings of increased competence, boosted arousal, and heightened understanding. It would appear that our species isn't called *Homo sapiens* for nothing!

Despite the satisfactions possible from just noticing things and from actively using our knowledge to perceive our surroundings more insightfully, our normal awareness plans often drift into lazily ignoring much of the richness of the world. We get used to things, overlook much, and simply store knowledge without using it to enliven our perceptions. That's when deliberately calling up the kinds of plans presented in this section can come to the rescue.

Noticing Things
You *Normally Wouldn't*

Taking the role of a male, how would you view this? Now taking the role of a female, how do you look at it? Does taking the role of the other sex lead you to notice things you normally would not? Or how about taking other roles, such as a designer of clothing or window displays, a hairdresser, a thief, or a small child? As a follow-up to this little exercise with the photograph, right now look around you and see how many things you can find in the next minute or two that you have not noticed before. You can use role-taking as an aid, or just look for details, patterns, or changes that you hadn't previously been aware of. You might even play this as a game whose object is to find X-number of unnoticed things in a familiar place.

Deliberately looking for things you normally wouldn't notice is an easy way to provoke yourself to closer observation and renewed interest in your surroundings. You'll almost certainly begin to notice things that will pique your curiosity and make the world seem richer and more complex. Mentally taking on different roles is especially valuable as an aid. (Pretending to be a tourist, reporter, painter, or poet are particularly good ways to sharpen your observation and curiosity—and to help you see things as if for the first time.) In addition, though, you might simply look around for everything you can find that is moving in any way, or try to notice all the uses of a particular substance like wood or metal around you, or pay close attention to other people's nonverbal behavior, or concentrate on noticing all the sounds and smells you can. What other simple aids can you think of for helping you notice things you normally wouldn't?

Searching for *Boring* Things— and Then Looking for Something Interesting About Them

Does this scene or particular things in it strike you as boring at first glance? If boring items don't jump out at you right away, try looking more closely. Search the scene and select everything you can find that seems likely to be boring were you to spend a lot of time examining it or thinking about it. Then once you've made your selections of "candidates for boredom," try to prove yourself wrong! How many interesting things can you discover or think of about your selections? For instance, if you think one of the buildings is boring, see what happens if you try guessing what is going on (or has gone on) inside it? Or see if you can find anything aesthetically interesting about some details of its exterior, shadows on its surface, or whatever. Does thinking about the probable past and future of a seemingly boring item help make it a little more interesting? Or how about thinking of potential new uses for it, or even imagining that it is alive? Does it help simply to notice as many subtle details about it as you can? Challenge yourself! Don't quit until you really do find something interesting about whatever you thought would be most boring.

When something seems boring, our usual inclination is to ignore it, right? But if instead we turn this around and deliberately set out to find and to closely examine "boring" things, we can experience some interesting surprises. First, a careful search for boring things almost automatically turns up many unnoticed interesting things as well. Then a close-up examination and imaginative exploration of the candidates for boredom will lead you to discover new things about them, and they may start to seem interesting after all. Just to be sure, though, make it a point to prove yourself wrong about the things you thought would be boring. Find something, anything, that is in fact interesting about them.

You can also turn this into a productive game with other people. One person challenges the others to find something interesting in an

object or event (say, waiting in line) that strikes the chooser as hopelessly boring. The other players then work on finding something that the chooser will admit is really interesting about it. (The person who suggests the most interesting aspect becomes the next chooser.) This sort of thing can easily have practical applications in addition to entertainment value—say, for helping students help each other to appreciate "dull" subjects.

Figuring Out
What the Things and Places
Around You *Communicate*

What "messages" does this entryway send to you? Specifically, what types of feelings or moods does it arouse? What impressions does it seem designed to create? Do you think particular types of behavior would be elicited by such a doorway? Does the doorway itself seem to express some kind of feeling? If this portal were an invitation or command, what would it be? For what sorts of buildings would such an entry be appropriate? How would your impression be affected if you saw this doorway on (a) a private house, (b) an elementary school, (c) a department store, (d) a courthouse, (e) the cover of a book?

To help you become more aware of how the environment can shape your behavior and feelings, ask yourself what messages are being communicated by buildings, landscaping, furniture, pathways, signs, and other objects and places around you. What types of behavior or feelings are elicited by the specific design or layout of your home, workplace, or street? What impressions do you think particular materials, interior designs, window displays, and vehicles are intended to create on passersby or users? What *un*intended messages are being communicated as well? See if you can even find some "false fronts"—mismatches between surface appearances and inside realities (such as an ultra-modern-looking school with a reactionary educational policy).

Thinking About
the Probable *Past and Future*
of Things You Notice

What guesses would you make about the past and future of this camper? See how far back you can go in figuring out its probable origins, including even the manufacturing process, the source of materials, and so on. Similarly, how far into the future can you follow its lifeline and eventual dissolution? What cues can you draw on from the camper and its surroundings to help you guess where it has gone and will go, and how it has been and will be used? By letting a vision of the whole past and future of this camper flash across your mind at once, you can start to see the camper as an *event* rather than as an object frozen in one moment of time.

Thinking about the lifelines of things around you can be very helpful for realizing that every "thing" really is an event occurring over time. This awareness plan can also help you to appreciate environmental sources and consequences of the items in your surroundings. It can even lead you to a better understanding of how intertwined everything on earth actually is. Finally, trying to guess the pasts and futures of things (and people) is a great way to test your knowledge and powers of observation—and to increase your curiosity.

Thinking of Something as the *Title of a Book* and Imagining What the Book Might Include

What might be in a book entitled *The Typewriter*? Offhand, you might think of topics like the history of typewriters, current typewriter technology, the nature of companies that produce these machines, fads and fashions in typewriter styles, effects typewriters have on various kinds of jobs and on communication, and so on. Or you might imagine a book about the particular typewriter shown in the picture, perhaps written as an imaginary autobiography about its feelings concerning the people who have used it and the things it has typed (including this book, for instance!). Or you might let your imagination roam farther afield to imagine *The Typewriter* as the title of a mystery, a ghost story, a science-fiction adventure, an exposé of goings-on in a secretarial pool, or an account of someone with a self-image as a machine spouting other people's thoughts. You might even think of *The Typewriter* as it would be in different sections of a bookstore or library. Filed under music, for instance, it might detail some strange uses for typewriters. Under sports, the book might discuss speed typing as the newest event at the Olympics. Under psychology, you might find something on the psychological effects of typing versus writing by hand. What other types of books could *The Typewriter* be?

In a similar way, you can envision books based on absolutely anything you choose. The possibilities are truly endless: *The Beer Bottle, Lost Dogs, Fighting at Home, Silly Ideas, Stuffy Rooms, Stuffy People, Book Titles.* . . . Try it right now with whatever catches your eye first. Think of its name or a short description as the title of a book and then let your imagination go to work. What would be in the book? How many different types of books could be written with that title? How much do you know that might go into such books? What interesting questions does thinking about this sort of book raise for you? You can use this awareness plan both to stimulate your curiosity and to boost your appreciation of how much you know about the world already.

Some Additional Awareness Plans for "Tuning In"

- Picking out all the items around you that seem to represent or symbolize a particular feeling, value, activity, idea, or state of being.

- Envisioning what's going on inside each thing you notice.

- Noticing all the human activities you can find.

- Figuring out people's probable relations with each other.

- Looking for subtle external clues about what people are really like (the "Sherlock Holmes" awareness plan).

- Figuring out possible political significance for everything you can.

- Looking for recurring cycles of activities or events; also looking for any repetitive patterns in your life or surroundings.

- Making (and checking) predictions about what is going to happen around you in the next few seconds, minutes, or (if you're daring) hours.

- Thinking of how various items in your environment use, store, generate, or transmit energy.

- Thinking of how social, political, and economic practices affect the way energy is used around you.

- Contemplating how things and practices you notice help to satisfy or block various human needs and desires.

- Thinking about what you would most like to know about the people or things you encounter.

• Randomly picking out any two items or events around you and figuring out how they are similar to each other.

• Relating everything you notice to some academic subject, such as history, ecology, or law; or relating everything you can to a special hobby or interest of yours.

———————————

○ What additional plans for tuning in can you add?

EVALUATING

The focus now shifts from observing things and applying your knowledge to the world to *evaluating* what you find. Evaluating is simply judging something in relation to some standard or criterion. The most general, important, and widespread type of evaluating is probably judging how "good" or "bad" something is. This, as you know, takes many forms and depends on your specific purposes and values. You can judge the "goodness" of a meal, for instance, on the basis of how good it tastes, how nutritious it is, how pleasant the company and atmosphere are, and any number of other criteria. However, there are many other possible ways to evaluate something besides how good or bad it seems, as the following awareness plans will illustrate. One of the beauties of our minds is that we can consciously choose what basis or criterion to use in making evaluations.

Although most of us are probably spontaneously evaluating much of the time, you may find it a very eye-opening exercise to *deliberately* evaluate in different ways. You can thus give yourself a sense of control over this often subconscious process and also expand your awareness of alternative standards you might use. In addition, just about any special awareness plan to evaluate things can increase your insight into problems, comparisons, and gradations among the items in your world.

Using *Unusual Units* of Comparison to Evaluate People and Things Around You

What traits or characteristics could a shark's jaws be used to measure? How about talkativeness or big-mouthedness, for instance? ("Jovial Jack jumps from two to six shark jaws after the first round of drinks.") Hunger would certainly seem a possibility, as would meanness. ("When I'm over three shark jaws hungry, I'm at least eight shark jaws mean!") Or you might use shark jaws to measure holes in someone's logic, the bitingness of pieces of gossip, or the degree to which prices "rip you off." Take a few minutes and see how many other things you can potentially evaluate in terms of shark jaws. In each case, how does using this unusual unit of measurement lead you to feel about what you are evaluating?

The main purpose of this awareness plan is to help you increase your insight and amusement about people, events, and things around you. It is especially helpful for making judgments about characteristics that are normally hard to quantify, since you compare things you are judging to a concrete example of some sort. Just make up a unit of measurement based on someone or something that strikes you as having a noteworthy characteristic, and you're in business. If, for instance, you know a fellow named Fred who has an exceptional sense of humor, try evaluating other people on how many "Fred" units of humor they seem to have. Perhaps Ralph will come out as only a fifth of a Fred, while Lily Tomlin might tip your scale at a whopping six Freds. Or a particularly gaudy clothing store might suggest a unit of gaudiness (a "gaud") that you could apply to clothing, buildings, billboards, and other things as well. Even if you never actually use the units you think of, just coming up with unusual ways to evaluate should be good for a smile along with some added insight and interest.

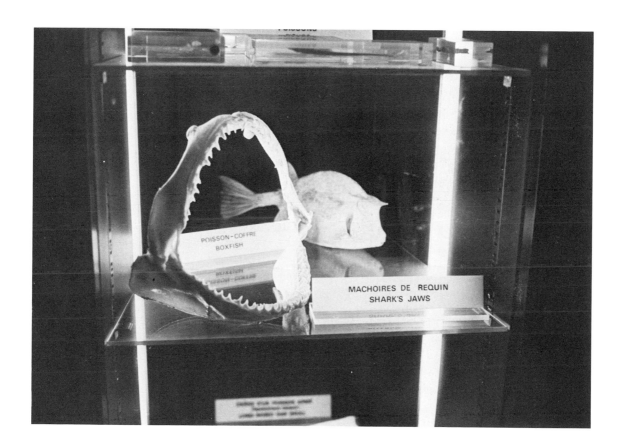

Looking at the World Through
Different Value Systems

Notice how this scene seems to change as you take on, in turn, the values that would likely be held by

    (1) a daredevil race car driver
    (2) an environmental lawyer
    (3) a blind pedestrian
    (4) a mad bomber
    (5) a _____ (fill in as you like).

As you try each of these roles, go ahead and exaggerate the values you associate with it. As a daredevil racer, imagine that things like speed, thrills, and danger are the only values of real importance. As a mad bomber, pretend that blowing things up is what life is all about. How does each role lead you to shift what you notice and think about while looking at the scene? What are the weirdest values you can think of for imaginary use here? (Some sample candidates: What if smoke were the most important thing in life? Or straight lines? Or letters of the alphabet? Or neighborliness?)

The basic idea here is to think of alternative types of values and view the world as if each value (in turn) were the most important thing in your life. As you switch among the different values, notice how your attention and thoughts change to accord with whatever value you're pretending is uppermost. This sort of self-observation while taking on new mental roles is especially helpful for developing empathy with the perspectives of other people. To maximize your flexibility in switching value perspectives, try moving between a particular value and its opposite. You might, for instance, first think of competition as the spice of life and then shift to regarding cooperation as the highest value. Or you could first take on the value system of a historian (preservation of the past?) and then switch to the values of a future-oriented land developer.

Engaging in
an *Orgy of Evaluation*

To demonstrate to yourself how easy it is to evaluate just about anything in just about any way you can think of, try this: Pick an item from Column 1 and use any criterion from Column 2 to evaluate it. Let's say, for example, that you pick Furniture from Column 1 and Fun from Column 2. Then try gauging how much fun each item of furniture in your house is. The TV set and the bed might rank very high, the kitchen chairs rather low, the lamps in between, and so on. Or maybe you matched Jobs and Natural vs. artificial. Here you might gauge how much any particular job involves working with natural vs. artificial things. Forest management would be highly natural, auto assembly line work very artificial, medicine a mixture, and so on.

The idea here is to explore the immense variety of ways to evaluate anything you might encounter in the world. Evaluation certainly need not be limited to a single dimension such as "good/bad," the most common type of judgment. Indeed, the more offbeat ways you can find to evaluate things around you, the more interesting and rich you're likely to find the world. For a start, see how many personally interesting items you can add to each column on the facing page.

COLUMN 1	COLUMN 2
Sample Things to Evaluate	*Sample Criteria for Evaluating*
Jobs	Fun
Buildings	Safety (or danger)
Organizations	Suitability for a vacation
Food	Contribution to survival
Furniture	Contribution to health
Electrical appliances	Natural vs. artificial
Recreational activities	Ephemeral vs. permanent
Books	Appeal to people of various ages
Television programs	Cost (or expensive vs. cheap)
Vehicles	Age (or old vs. new)
Toys	Real vs. pretend or fake
Weather conditions	Active vs. passive
Friends or acquaintances	Flexibility
Yourself	Odd vs. usual

Figuring Out
the *Cultural Values* Implied
by Things Around You

What values, goals, and patterns of culture would give rise to this scene? Think carefully about all that is contained here. What does this one scene tell you about our culture's values, views of human nature, styles of recreation, and the like? Which of these cultural patterns would you personally evaluate as especially good and which as especially bad? Why? What do your own answers reveal about values your culture has passed on to you?

This is a challenging awareness plan, calling for close observation of your surroundings and serious thought about the implications of the activities and things you notice. What kinds of values and goals would lead us to act as we have and to produce the things that we find around us? You might even try thinking of yourself as an anthropologist from another culture who is here on a field trip. What conclusions and guesses would you make about what this culture holds dear? What common things and events do you think provide the best clues to our society's basic values?

SECTION V

IMAGINING
IMPROVEMENTS

So far you have moved from fanciful reinterpretation through aesthetic appreciation to tuning in on various meanings and evaluations of things around you. The step awaiting you now is to consider things as you would *like* them to be. This will call once again on your powers of creative imagination, but now with a focus on visions of desirable future possibilities rather than on pure fantasy. You should find, though, that the playful flexibility, aesthetic appreciation, and sharpened insight you have experienced with earlier awareness plans will contribute nicely to your ability to imagine beneficial changes in anything you pick.

It of course isn't very rare for most of us to imagine improvements in our lives or our surroundings. Notice how often you think about such matters as improving your working conditions, changing someone's behavior, redecorating your home, or even setting the government or the environment straight. What may be rare is to deliberately set out to form mental images of such improvements and to employ special creativity aids to help generate better ideas. That, along with the goal of figuring out ways to achieve the improvements, is what this section is all about.

Imagining Improvements
in *Problem Spots* Around You

It's usually not hard to find "problem places" you would like to see improved. Can you think of such a spot in your own house or neighborhood, for instance? (It need not be in quite the dire straits shown here, though!) Once you've thought of a place that could use some improvement, how many positive changes can you envision off the top of your head? These changes can be as wild and sweeping as you like, but imagine each change as *vividly* as you can—really form a clear mental image of what the improvements would be like.

This is the first step in a series of mental activities designed to help you become more practiced and creative in imagining improvements in your world. This sort of imaginative awareness not only provides interesting mental stimulation, but also adds to your sense of creativity and competence, alerts you to problems and possibilities in whatever you focus on, and prepares you to take constructive action.

Imagining Improvements
in Already *Pleasant Things*
Around You

Now, for a little more challenge, what kinds of improvements can you imagine for some *pleasant* place without any obvious problems, such as a nice beach? (Or pick some especially nice part of your house, neighborhood, or city, and see if you can manage to imagine ways it could be still better.) Again, form as clear and vivid a mental image of each improvement as you can. Also, set yourself to think up several different types of improvements rather than just one or two. Each can be as sweeping and impractical as you like, however.

It is generally harder to come up with beneficial changes for things we regard as already very good than for problem spots. But if you can manage to envision improvements in a pleasant thing, your ideas are likely to be fairly creative. The challenge and novelty of thinking up ways to make a good thing even better seem to spur us to generate unusual notions. If you find yourself having trouble at this point, though, the creativity aids coming up shortly should prove especially useful.

Thinking up *Actions*
That Would Lead to
Improvements You Imagine

If you really wanted to achieve some of the changes you imagined for the last two awareness plans, what might you actually be able to do? Here is where creative thought is surely at a premium, since figuring out effective action strategies is generally much harder than envisioning changes. As a first step, try working backward from your envisioned improvement. What actions or state of affairs would be needed as the *last* phase of a plan to achieve the change? What actions would have to precede that phase, and on down the line? For instance, if you imagined a vibrant new playground for your neighborhood, the final phase of an action plan would be the actual construction of the park. Preceding that would be allocation of funds by the city government or perhaps a commitment by a neighborhood association to work on the playground. Prior to that might be a lobbying effort, seeking a referendum, or forming the neighborhood association. As you follow this process of working backward, you should eventually find a stage where *you* can enter as a participant in working for the final goal.

As an alternative approach for thinking up actions, you might start by listing the various things you can do that could conceivably contribute to your goal. Mentally follow through by thinking of the consequences each type of action might have. Then simply pick the approach that seems most promising and begin there.

Creativity Aids
for Imagining Improvements
and Actions

The twelve creativity aids summarized on the facing page can help you to do a variety of things characteristic of creative thinking. These include breaking your usual assumptions; flexibly taking on new points of view; thinking of unusual combinations and connections; generating a large number of new ideas; and thinking in terms of positive possibilities as well as mere correction of problems. As you come to each of the aids in the next few pages, you'll gain most skill and remember the aid most easily if you immediately try it out. Use each aid to help you imagine improvements in something and think of actions to achieve these improvements. Although a dozen main techniques are offered, even one or two of them can be enough to help out on a particular problem. Experiment to see which ones work best for you.

---

1. Think of everything you can that helps you to be creative. After making a list of as many items as possible, vividly imagine what it feels like to experience these things.

As a sample list, you may find that your creativity is boosted by

being playful	not worrying about criticism
relaxing	nonverbal thinking
being confident	exercising
feeling energetic	reading poetry
trying to be absurd	becoming immersed in the
feeling independent	problem
not straining	using new awareness plans...

What other things can you think of that have been especially helpful to *your* creativity? Can you put yourself in a creative frame of mind simply by imagining or remembering what it feels like to experience these things?

2. Use "What if...?" questions that challenge your usual assumptions or expectations. If you're imagining improvements in your living room, for instance, try asking questions like the following to help you envi-

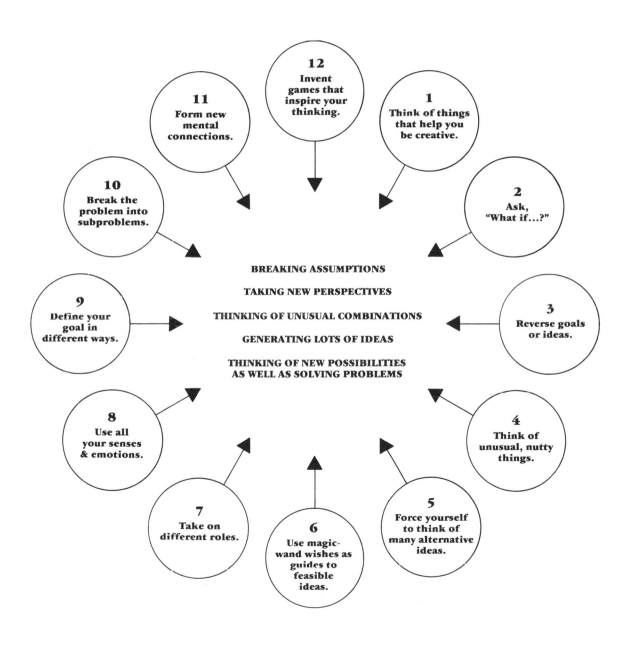

12 Invent games that inspire your thinking.

11 Form new mental connections.

1 Think of things that help you be creative.

10 Break the problem into subproblems.

2 Ask, "What if…?"

9 Define your goal in different ways.

3 Reverse goals or ideas.

8 Use all your senses & emotions.

4 Think of unusual, nutty things.

7 Take on different roles.

6 Use magic-wand wishes as guides to feasible ideas.

5 Force yourself to think of many alternative ideas.

BREAKING ASSUMPTIONS

TAKING NEW PERSPECTIVES

THINKING OF UNUSUAL COMBINATIONS

GENERATING LOTS OF IDEAS

THINKING OF NEW POSSIBILITIES AS WELL AS SOLVING PROBLEMS

sion goals: What if nothing could rest on the floor? What if the room had two levels? What if I designed the room to make fighting fun? What if only blind people were going to use the room? Then use your questions to help you generate interesting ideas for actual changes—perhaps things like hanging decorations from the ceiling, building a mezzanine of sorts, or relying mainly on soft furniture.

Similarly, you might ask "What if" questions to help you figure out creative actions. Some sample questions might be: What if I could spend no money to achieve this change? What if I doubled (or cut in half) the time I could wait for the change? What if I viewed things that seemed to block my change as potentially positive forces? What if everything I did for this change had to be fun? What if this change were truly the most important thing in my life?

3. Explore reversals of your goals or ideas. For example, think of how you might make your living room *worse*. Can you then reverse the ideas you come up with and thereby think of innovative improvements? Or as you think of any particular improvement, such as adding more colorful drapes, try reversing the idea: perhaps taking the drapes away altogether and devising other ways to cover or decorate the windows.

For thinking of action strategies, you could imagine that you were working against your goal. Does this give you some insight into some of the opposing forces and how you might deal with them constructively? Say you want to make your marriage more harmonious. How would you act if your goal were to increase conflict instead? Now can you imagine how to reverse those actions so as to increase harmony? Or when you think of a potential action to achieve some goal, try thinking of how reversals of the action might also be useful. If, for instance, you think of boycotting the products of a company to try to change its policies, you might also think of buying its products (or even its stock) to establish yourself as someone with a personal stake in seeing the company change positively—as a friendly change agent rather than an adversary.

4. Deliberately set out to think of unusual, even nutty, things. How many ridiculous ways can you think of to redecorate your living room? What, for instance, are some truly unusual floor coverings you can think of? What's the weirdest furniture you can imagine? What are some off-the-wall activities you can envision for your living room, and how would the room be set up for each activity? How might you combine floors with doors?…Now, do your answers suggest anything that might be a starting place for genuinely useful ideas that nonetheless depart from your old assumptions?

Using "What if ?" questions and also reversing some of your ideas, what way-out changes can you think of to make in the design of subway cars? How might you push these thoughts further and envision improvements in the whole system of mass transit in cities?

On the action side, you can similarly call on zany notions to suggest feasible assumption-breakers. Let's say you want your child's school to have a more interesting playground. What are some ridiculous ideas for action—giving up your job to work full-time on the playground? hypnotizing all the kids to think the playground is already improved? selling off the school building to provide money for the playground? applying for a federal grant?... Assuming none of these ideas will work as is, what feasible actions can you dig out of your far-fetched notions? Perhaps parents, kids, and teachers could work part-time on renovating the playground. Perhaps the kids might really be encouraged to make more imaginative use of the existing facilities. Maybe some way could be found to rent out parts of the school building at night or over the summer and thus raise money for playground improvements. Perhaps a special physical education research project could be proposed that would indeed merit a federal grant.

5. Force yourself to come up with lots of alternative ideas. The first run of ideas will likely clear out cliché notions (paint the walls a different color, get new rugs) and pave the way for imagined improvements that open new vistas and break old assumptions. Why not pick something you would like to improve, and right now try to think up ten alternative changes that would help?

In using this technique as an aid for envisioning action strategies, you'll also do best if you make each new action as different as possible from the others you think up. Thus, if you've already imagined six ways to make money for a change you'd like, try for a seventh action that contributes to the change but has nothing to do with money—say, that involves changing attitudes or recycling materials already on hand.

6. Imagine you have a magic wand. What changes or actions would you use the wand to create, especially things that wouldn't normally be possible to achieve? After letting your fancy run wild for a while, ask yourself what specific features of these magical wishes particularly appeal to you. Then try to figure out feasible changes or actions that actually embody some of these specific features. Starting with the magic wand should help you get away from old assumptions, and the follow-up steps will help you build on your expanded vision.

Suppose your magical wish is to have your living room perched high in the Rocky Mountains. Let's say the specific things you like about this are the view, the quiet and solitude, the crisp mountain air, and the feeling of openness. You might get at some of these features even in a cramped urban apartment by hanging appropriate posters or paintings, getting stereo headphones, and installing special air conditioning.

Or if your goal were to think of actions to get your boss to be more open to employees' suggestions, you might start by imagining that you could spike her morning coffee with a magical open-mindedness pill. This would have such advantages as being effortless, hassle-free, sure, simple, nonthreatening to all concerned, and speedy. Are there any real actions that might have some of these features? Perhaps anonymously giving the boss a book like Thomas Gordon's *Leader Effectiveness Training* would come close, since this is a way to convey the advantages and skills of open-mindedness. Or maybe if employees gift-wrapped

How many very different nutty ways to improve committee meetings can you think up in the next five minutes?

their suggestions and slipped them to the boss as morning presents, that would get through on occasion. Can you think of other actions that could resemble a "magic pill" in their effect?

7. Take on different roles as you imagine improvements. For example, what sorts of changes in your living room do the following roles suggest: garbage collector (more interesting trash baskets? use found objects as furniture or decorations?); botanist (more plants? put in a skylight? a small fountain to humidify the air?); historian (add reminders of the best past places you've visited or lived in?); lawyer (more order?); toddler (softer rugs? more interesting moving things?)? Taking on new roles is a nearly magical creativity aid. It's fun and effective—and can be carried pretty far. How, for instance, would an electric fan think of improving your living room (wind chimes? airy drapes? more extension cords or wall outlets?)? And what suggestions might be offered by a potted plant, a tape recorder, or a piece of cheese?

This technique is just as effective in the realm of devising actions. Let's say you're looking for ways to help you accomplish a change in yourself, such as quitting smoking. What ideas for actions can you suggest to yourself, taking the role (in turn) of a watchmaker, a pianist, an embezzler, a poet, and, if you feel daring, a movie camera or an ice cube? (A suggestion that springs to my mind in the watchmaker role is to take a cigarette carefully apart and then try to put it back together grain by grain every time the urge to smoke hits. As an ice cube, I think of imagining my lungs melting away if I take a puff, or perhaps soaking my hand in cold water to take my mind off a nicotine fit. But, then, I'm not a smoker.)

8. Use different senses and emotions to suggest new possibilities. In living room redesign, for instance, touch may suggest the use of new textures or creating a closer, friendlier atmosphere. Taste may lead you to ideas for new places to eat in your living room. Anger may suggest more flamboyant, vibrant colors and arrangements. Joy might lead you to ideas for more carefree and simple living. And so on. It helps, when using senses and emotions as spurs to creativity, to form the most vivid impression you can of the sensations and feelings you select.

Turning to the domain of action, let's say your goal is to increase excitement and harmony at your place of work. Sight might suggest using posters, photographs, or pantomime as aids. Smell could point to strategies like using incense as an atmosphere setter at a meeting. And again, the full range of human emotions—from humor and joy to sadness and anger—can be used as points of departure. What is the funniest tactic you can think of to achieve some change you'd like? How might you constructively channel anger into an attack on a problem instead of on people? Could the active expression of sadness be used to move toward a beneficial goal, as in the case of newsworthy candlelight vigils to protest some impending social or environmental harm?

9. Define your problem (goal) in many different ways. For example, improving your living room might be thought of as (a) making the place more attractive and comfortable just for you, (b) turning it into something suitable for a *House Beautiful* photograph, (c) finding the best arrangement for what is already there, (d) figuring out the best remodeling job you could do for X-number of dollars, and on and on. Or if you were seeking action strategies to help improve water quality in your community, you might alternatively define your action goals as (a)

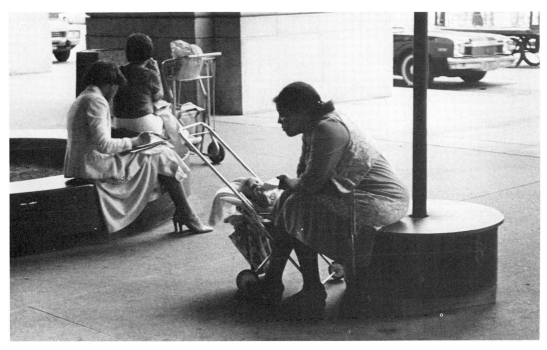

What imagined roles do you think would be most helpful to your creativity for figuring out ways to improve child-rearing?

What feelings does this scene arouse for you? See if you can use these feelings as springboards for thinking up possible improvements in a vacation you might take (and for coming up with actions that would make this vacation possible!).

effecting change as fast as possible, (b) getting the maximum number of people interested in achieving the change, (c) raising funds for the improvements, (d) collecting as many alternative plans as possible, and so forth. Whether you're envisioning goals or means, each new definition of purpose will point your thinking toward new possibilities.

10. Break the problem into subproblems. If you find it hard to think of ways to achieve your whole goal, try focusing on one part at a time and think of changes or actions that would contribute to each part. Also, once you've thought of a potential improvement or action, try breaking it down into subparts and see if you can think of ways to better each of these.

In thinking up ways to improve your living room, you might focus in turn on potential improvements for each separate area of the room or type of furniture. Or you might break down the problem in terms of finding improvements for each type of activity that occurs in the living room. In figuring out action strategies for, say, improving the physical fitness of your family, you could focus on such "subparts" as buying or finding access to exercise equipment, studying about nutrition, experimenting with different sleep schedules, planning more active recreation and vacations, and so on. The more subparts you can think of, the better your chances are to come up with creative new possibilities.

11. Form new mental connections. The simplest way to do this is to think of things or situations that are in some way similar to what it is you want to change or do, and use them as new points of departure for your thinking. In improving your living room, you might think of a restaurant or hotel lobby you especially liked, and use it as a model. Or you might go farther afield and try to derive ideas from museums, parks, or bird nests. You can even pick things that are decidedly not to your liking (perhaps a jail cell or bus terminal) and use a *reversal* of their features as a source of inspiration. You can similarly use new mental connections to think of new actions. If you're trying to increase friendliness in your workplace, for instance, try thinking of how friendly groups you've known in the past created and maintained their good feelings. Or think of analogies from nature. Symbiotic relations and other types of mutual aid among animals and plants might give you some ideas for effective actions with your colleagues.

To push your thinking still further, simply take anything that comes to mind and try to connect it to your goal. What do glaciers suggest for remodeling your living room? (Some possible loose connections: air conditioning; glass sculptures; very slow changes; highly reflective surfaces and walls to brighten the room; easily movable, "slippery" furniture.) Or what ideas do socks or speeding trucks bring up for your living room?

In the realm of action, you can often generate productive ideas by trying to link in something you already enjoy doing. For instance, if your goal were to make your neighborhood safer for people to walk at night, how might you use a hobby, such as playing bridge, as a means? (Perhaps you could organize a bridge tournament to raise money for improved street lighting, or stage an outdoor "bridge-in" to draw public attention to your cause.) Or could you use the activities involved in playing bridge to suggest creative actions for street safety? Perhaps ideas will come to mind like having partners to walk with, stashing spades

Starting with elegant restaurants, what ideas come to mind for creative actions to achieve a beneficial change you desire in yourself?

and clubs around, or taking turns being "dummy" and watching the street.

12. Invent imaginative games that can inspire your thinking. By combining imaginative and playful activities with your problem-solving, you will likely spin off more original ideas. Games can also make it easier and more fun to use several creativity aids on the same problem. Here, for instance, is a possible game for helping you imagine (and create) improvements for your living room:

Phase 1: Gather everyone who lives with you into the living room and explain the procedure.

Phase 2: Ask each other "What if...?" questions for about five minutes (to loosen up assumptions about what can be done with the living room).

Phase 3: Spend a few minutes taking on animal roles and telling how each of you, from your animal's perspective, would most like to see the room changed.

Phase 4: See how many of these animal suggestions you can use to generate feasible ideas for making the room more pleasant for yourselves as you really are.

Phase 5: Invent a new game whose object would be helping you come up with creative actions to achieve the changes from Phase 4. An example might be having each person make up a wild idea for action and then challenge everyone else to build on it to suggest something realistic. Or you could even start by making it a game to see who can invent the best game to help devise effective actions.

What games might an alligator think up to inspire creative ideas for your living room?

BASIC ENLIGHTENMENT

Y ou have been developing a diversity of skills for perceiving in more flexible and creative ways. You are likely more adept now at using your imagination to break away from mundane interpretations and to see the world afresh—whether fancifully, aesthetically, or with heightened awareness and insight. Moreover, you have been exploring techniques to be more creative in envisioning improvements and inventing strategies for achieving these improvements. The purpose of the current section is to provide a few potent and encompassing awareness plans to help you integrate all that you have gained and use it more effectively to enjoy life to the fullest. The underlying state of mind to develop is what I am calling "basic enlightenment."

Now *enlightenment* has many meanings, most of which involve a spiritual or religious connotation. It is often thought of as a state of fantastically expanded consciousness, oneness with God or universal consciousness, and unimaginable bliss. I certainly have no objections to such a state of being, but I am here thinking of enlightenment as simply a way of experiencing that maximizes your joy and fulfillment starting right now rather than as a transcendent goal that may take more than one lifetime to achieve. What follows, then, is some advice on how you might begin immediately to experience each moment of your life in potentially richer and more fulfilling ways.

Thinking of Every Moment as an *Opportunity*

One of the best ways to expand and activate your choices in life is simply to remind yourself that every moment really is an opportunity for choosing ways to experience and to act. For any situation, just say to yourself: "OK, this is what I have to work with. Now what am I going to do with it? How am I going to experience it? I am committed to treat *this situation* as an opportunity for a fulfilling and constructive experience." Remember also that your situation always includes your own thoughts and feelings as well as the external circumstances of your life. So if you are facing, say, a depressing event, the "opportunity" involves not only how you will treat the event itself but also how you will treat your feelings of depression. (Notice, for instance, that if you were writing a book about depression, you might very easily regard feeling depressed as a genuine opportunity to gather firsthand information for your work.)

Although this awareness plan applies to all situations, you may find it especially useful for reinterpreting circumstances you view as problematic or disturbing. Try asking yourself how you could turn a family argument into an opportunity for personal growth or for coming up with creative ways to resolve conflict. Or see if you can think of positive opportunities provided by rainy days, colds, broken appliances, inflation, or other everyday sources of what we usually view as frustrations. If you will take a single problem that has been bugging you and spend a half-hour or so thoroughly exploring possible opportunities that it might provide for enriching your life, you may give yourself a very pleasant surprise.

Regarding Whatever You're Doing, Thinking, or Feeling as if It Were Your *Hobby*

Imagine that you're washing those dishes over there across the page— and that it's a drag, as usual, to wash dishes. Now see if you can change this by thinking of washing dishes as a longstanding hobby of yours. First, you can warm up by thinking of just how it feels to engage in a hobby you genuinely enjoy. The hobby might be a sport, art or craft, reading, collecting, or whatever. Just get clearly in mind the feelings and mental activities you associate with hobbies—perhaps intense interest, aesthetic delight, feelings of choosing to do what you're doing, loving the activity, paying close attention to everything about it, and the like. Then transfer at least an echo of these feelings and ways of thinking to the activity of washing those dishes. Can you do this—imagine that washing dishes is really a hobby, something you look forward to, take pride in, savor, know the fine points of, do for recreation, and so on? How would this change your experience when washing real dishes?

If it is hard for you to treat washing dishes itself as an enjoyable pastime, and especially if you strongly dislike washing dishes, perhaps you can regard *hating it* as your hobby. You might think to yourself, "Oh boy, here's another chance to hate washing dishes; I'll explore all the fine nuances of how I hate it this time. . . ."

With a little practice and determination, you should be able to generate some "hobby feeling" for just about any activity you choose. Fairly neutral things, like brushing your teeth, reading the morning paper, walking the dog, or driving to work, may be easiest for starters. But even an illness or a task you genuinely dislike can be fair game for this awareness plan. As pointed out, you can always fall back on treating your dislike itself as your real hobby! Ultimately, the value of this awareness plan is to brighten up your life and help you realize that you can always choose to be doing or feeling whatever you actually are doing or feeling.

Thinking of Things
You Can *Learn* From
Whatever You Encounter

What sorts of things could strolling through a cemetery give you a chance to learn? Additionally, how could you treat your own and other people's reactions to cemeteries as an opportunity to teach yourself something?

———————————

Regarding everything as having something important to teach you is an especially powerful and positive awareness plan. However, you'll get the most out of it if you actively seek some way you can learn from things rather than waiting for them to "teach" you. In taking this active approach, be ready to suspend your assumptions about what is relevant and important, try out unusual mental roles (such as asking what the residents might learn from cemetery visitors), and look for new connections and relationships among things around you. Be especially on the lookout for opportunities to learn from unusual sources— perhaps your subordinates or children, covers of record albums, clouds, the contents of garbage cans, TV commercials. And see also what you can learn from your own emotions, thoughts, and behavior. Just about every thing and occurrence in life can be mined for some educational value if you'll do some mental digging.

For Any Problematic Situation, Focusing on What You Are Doing and Especially What *You Can Do*

Can you see this photograph as a metaphor for something in your own life—for some situation where you feel trapped or put upon? If so, try asking yourself what exactly *you* are doing—and more important, what you can do—rather than focusing on what you see as being done to you. Being as creative as you can, what are some possible actions that would help you make constructive changes in the situation or extricate yourself from it? Even if you can't change the situation itself, can you think of some new ways to experience it that would make a positive difference in how you feel? (As one example, what would happen if you stopped resisting and treated the whole thing as a game or as an educational experience? Might this even in turn suggest some actions you hadn't thought of?)

The secret to effective use of this approach to experiencing difficult situations is to emblazon in your mind that you *do* have options about how you are going to act and think. For a situation you want to change, start by committing yourself to finding something—*anything*—that you yourself can do to make a difference. At times this may come down to no more than choosing to experience the situation with a new awareness plan, such as a playful or aesthetic one to ease your discomfort. With creativity and a bit of determination, though, consistently asking what you can do may well turn up a wealth of meaningful actions where before lay only frustration.

Regarding Everything as *Perfect* Exactly the Way It Is Each Moment

To get some practice in seeing things as "perfect"—complete, totally fitting, just right—simply pick some ordinary thing or situation and brainstorm all the reasons you can think of for its perfection. Something you view as messy, such as dirty clothes strewn all over your bedroom, can provide a good place to start. Why might such a mess be considered perfect? Well, maybe it is exactly in keeping with your lifestyle or with your mood. Perhaps it perfectly conveys a feeling of nonchalance and of relaxed living. Your particular mess might serve as a perfect symbol of your privacy, and also provide a flawlessly beautiful array of colors, shapes, and shadows. No matter what, it can be seen as a perfect example of a *genuine* mess. And it may even strike you as a perfect reminder to do the laundry (in which case being bothered by the mess becomes part of its perfection).

For some general guidelines to finding perfection:

- Anything is always totally appropriate to being what it is; it is always a perfect example of itself. (You, for instance, are the perfect *you*.)

- When facing something that upsets you, such as an illness or injustice, you can mentally back off and include your own reaction to the situation as part of your overall awareness. This can help you find some value, and even perfection, in the fittingness of your reaction to the situation (as in being bothered by the dirty clothes).

- By temporarily relaxing and assuming that everything really is perfect, you can begin to feel a certain "rightness" about things like the mess—a sense that these clothes, at *this* moment, do indeed belong just where they are. As you expand your horizons, you may even come to realize that same sense of complete appropriateness about the way everything in the universe fits together.

- Even if you have trouble regarding absolutely everything as perfect, this awareness plan could prove useful for little things that

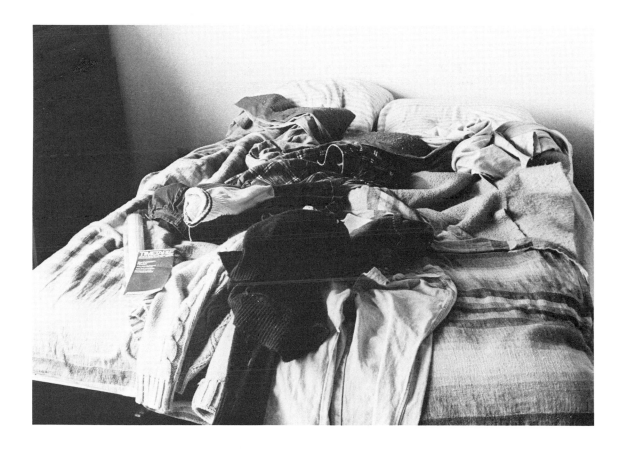

seem to go wrong. Rain on a hike, for example, might be perfect for giving you a chance to laugh at yourself, enjoy some gorgeous wet sights and sounds in the woods, exercise your skill at improvising shelter, and so on. The key is to be willing to make the unusual assumption that perfection is unfolding right before your eyes. Your commitment is then to think of reasons why this might be so and to appreciate those reasons.

* Finally, *change* can be viewed as perfect too—just in case you eventually pick up the clothes!

The Power of Meta-Awareness

The foregoing awareness plans are *powerful.* If you actually regard every moment as a new positive opportunity to exercise your choice about how to experience life—and if you sensitize yourself to the wealth of options you can create—the result can be incredibly energizing and satisfying. Each moment then actually does become an opportunity for enriching life in some way, for making it more lovable, if you will. Notice that if you so choose, you can equally make life into a drag by using a negative version of these plans. Just think of regarding everything as drudgery or as an insoluble problem, for instance. With such a negative orientation you might easily shut yourself off from enjoying or constructively reacting to *anything.* Being enlightened versus being stifled is a choice that is ours to make.

Each of the awareness plans in this section has encouraged you to step outside your immediate involvement in a situation to take a look at how you are experiencing it and to explore new possibilities. This process of stepping back to observe and reflect on your experience is what I call *meta-awareness.* Used creatively, it can enable you to find value in virtually any situation.

One underlying insight you can gain from meta-awareness is that you are not your thoughts, feelings, beliefs, sensations, or any other content of your experience. You are the *experiencer.* You can also be the chooser of how to experience. With these insights you may well find it possible to disentangle yourself from deep immersion in bouts of depression, anxiety, or anger. Rather than being totally caught up in such negative emotions, you can observe your feelings with equanimity and perhaps even find ways to use them to enrich rather than detract from the quality of life. At the very least, you might regard your feelings as a passing show where you are both actor and audience. And you can savor emotions like joy and humor all the more as you expand your consciousness to observe them even as you directly participate in these positive feelings. You may even come to value *experiencing,* whatever the specific content of your awareness, as a wondrous miracle to be appreciated every moment you're alive.

Stepping back to observe and choose your experiences also opens the way to what we might call *active acceptance*. As opposed to resignation or passive acceptance, active acceptance means searching out some way of experiencing or treating a situation so that you can say yes to it and genuinely mean it. For instance, you no doubt find things like starvation and child abuse abhorrent. Passive acceptance might involve throwing up your hands in apathetic resignation or shutting off your mind to the problem altogether. But active acceptance would flow from the meta-awareness that you can indeed say yes to the total situation of *your being dismayed* by starvation or child abuse. Even in the face of misfortunes and serious problems, you can still be glad that you are dismayed and want to take constructive action. Active acceptance thus in no way reduces your determination to change bad situations. But some of the sting and frustration is removed from life's troubles if you operate from a meta-aware point of view that enables you to find value in your reaction to circumstances even when you don't like the circumstances in themselves.

So I hope you will demonstrate to yourself by experimenting with the plans in this section that meta-awareness can free you to relax in the face of adversity and stress, to realize options for action and experience you might not otherwise think of, and to find greater joy, intensity, and value in each moment as you live it.

SECTION VII

SYNERGISTIC CONSCIOUSNESS

Now that we have come all the way from fanciful perception to basic enlightenment, a further step in this journey would be to think and act in creatively cooperative ways with other people. The mentality underlying this pattern of thinking and living I call *synergistic consciousness*. I believe it is a valuable ideal to aim for because such a frame of mind alerts us to our true interdependencies with each other and can stir us to create an ever more livable world. The awareness plans in this section are intended to illustrate synergistic ways of thinking and perceiving.

"Synergy" refers to combined action, where contributions reinforce each other. The word also connotes creativity and cooperation when it is applied to the way people interact with each other. As I see it, the essential ingredients in synergistic consciousness are thinking holistically, valuing the well-being of all people, and being eager to join with other people to come up with creative solutions to problems and disagreements. Holistic thinking involves an appreciation of how everything in the world, including yourself, is an interconnected whole. A synergistic orientation toward other people calls for honest communication, creative mutual problem-solving rather than win/lose approaches to conflicts, and inviting rather than forcing or manipulating other people to follow your ideas. When people act together in these ways, the odds are good that they will find goals and means that excite mutual, synergistic efforts by all concerned.

Contemplating
the Total *Situation*
in Which You Are Enmeshed

Consider that at any moment you are intertwined in some particular situation consisting of the people in your life, your physical surroundings, the tasks you perform, the news and entertainment you take in, and so forth. Right now notice how many aspects of this total "situation" you can bring to mind. Then begin to envision the situations of each of these parts of your own immediate situation. Think, for instance, of the friendships and tasks that your friends and family members have. These and other aspects of *their* situations affect the way they are—and hence the ways they affect you. You might even carry this a step or two further and think about the situations of your friends' friends. As you do this, you may well get the feeling that your own "situation" is like a ripple in a pond, intersecting and surrounded by other ripples in ever expanding circles.

Getting a sense of this vast network of overlapping, interconnected situations is a good way to impart to yourself a feeling of real connection even with people and things you do not encounter personally. Indeed, as a final exercise to show yourself that you are ultimately interconnected with *everything,* pick absolutely anything at all and figure out some way that it is part of your total situation and that you are part of its.

Defining Conflicts
in Terms of *Underlying Needs*
Instead of Incompatible Solutions

Think of a conflict with other people and imagine how you might handle it by figuring out ways to satisfy everyone's underlying needs or desires. Say, for instance, you and your roommate are battling over how loud to play the stereo. You love it loud, and your roommate wants it way down. If the two of you define this problem strictly in terms of preconceived solutions—like turning the sound up versus turning it down—the conflict may be very difficult to resolve to the satisfaction of both of you. What if, instead, you begin by determining what needs or desires underlie your preferences, and then define the problem as finding a way to meet these basic needs or desires. You might discover that your basic concern is to feel free to listen to raucous music, while your roommate needs quiet in order to read. If both of you were committed to finding a resolution that satisfied each of these needs, you might come up with possibilities like purchasing headphones, finding a mutually agreeable time for you to listen to music, or searching out pleasant alternative places to read or to hear loud music. The net result could be both satisfied needs and a strengthened friendship.

Focusing first on needs rather than on preconceived solutions could in fact do wonders for resolving many social conflicts. Just think of the possibilities for such issues as nuclear power plants, school busing, and welfare programs. With participants concentrating on meeting everyone's underlying goals, conflicting groups would have a much better chance to start proposing new, creative solutions. The key to success would be for everyone to enter the process with a firm commitment to find a solution that will work for all and to involve each other fully in divulging real needs and in developing potential solutions. Under these conditions it is very unlikely that people would trap themselves into narrow, polarizing views.

Looking for
Points in Other People's
Ideas to *Build On*

The next time you get into a discussion or argument with someone, flex your creativity by deliberately focusing on as many good points as you can find in the other's ideas and building on them to generate still better ideas. Let's say you're in a discussion about child-rearing and someone says that spanking is the best way to handle problems. If you disagree with this view, rather than immediately trying to tear down the other person's position, see if you can find *something* in his or her ideas that you can genuinely agree with or can use as a place to start for generating better ideas. Here, for instance, you might think that spanking is itself a mistake but agree with the idea of letting your children know when their behavior is unacceptable to you. You could then build on this positive aspect of spanking and start suggesting alternative, less punitive ways to achieve the same effect.

This awareness plan is based on the Spectrum Policy, a guiding principle of the highly effective group creativity procedure called "synectics." This principle, described by George Prince in his book *The Practice of Creativity,* is always to pick out the best part of the total spectrum of someone's ideas and to treat the weaker portions as challenges to be overcome rather than as points of attack or rejection. Maintaining this constructive, positive orientation both stimulates your own creativity and promotes a friendly, productive social atmosphere. All it takes is a commitment to finding and creating good ideas rather than proving you are right and someone else is wrong.

Thinking of Your Own and Other People's *Ideas as Gifts* or Invitations

So often in our culture we seem to think of arguing as if it were a kind of war. What if we shifted to viewing disagreements as if they were celebrations or parties of ideas? What if we thought of ourselves as living in a shared pool of thoughts rather than as "possessing" or originating ideas? What if we also thought of error or being wrong as simply an opportunity to learn rather than as a weakness to be attacked? And, most of all, what if we could think of our own goals or proposals as invitations to explore for even better ideas?

If we could but shift a few of our guiding assumptions and metaphors, we might discover that finding sharable, exciting goals and means does not have to be much of a struggle at all.

Thinking of *Superordinate Goals* That Would Resolve Conflicts and Excite Enthusiasm

A "superordinate goal" is a goal so big or exciting that people who were previously in conflict with each other, or who were apathetic, can enthusiastically unite to pursue it. Survival often provides the basis for superordinate goals, as when a community pulls together after a natural disaster or when nations unite against enemies during a war. But superordinate goals can also be based simply on seeking creative improvements in life. A low-income neighborhood in Philadelphia, for instance, once united in a highly cooperative, "superordinate" effort to help design and build their own community recreation area. Another example could be a bored family that excites and mobilizes itself to plan a tropical vacation. Discovering true superordinate goals requires that people communicate honestly with each other about what they really want. In addition, a strong commitment to creativity and continuous searching for better solutions helps a lot.

Right now, can you think of some creative and exciting aims that might serve as superordinate goals for you and your family, you and your co-workers, or you and your neighbors?

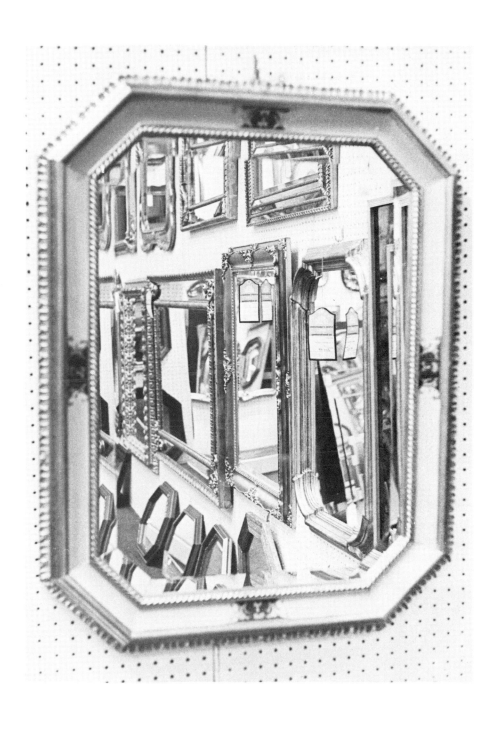

Some Additional Awareness Plans for Synergistic Consciousness

- Working out the links of a social, environmental, or even personal problem to our whole way of life in this society.

- Figuring out the "needs" that things around you must have satisfied in order to continue existing or to function properly.

- Imagining what it would feel like to be the entire universe.

- Thinking of all the interrelations you can that somehow connect things, people, and events around you to each other.

- Figuring out what activities in life are intrinsically enjoyable to you and other people, and then searching for basic things these activities have in common.

- Thinking carefully about how other people's happiness or unhappiness affects your own feelings and also how your state of mind comes to affect other people.

- Imagining changes in the world that would make it easier for all of us to experience life joyfully.

- Consciously taking other people's points of view, or perhaps even imagining that you *are* the people you encounter.

- Thinking of the advantages of sharing power and decision-making with other people.

- Viewing other people as "Origins"—as self-directing, responsible, choosing creatures.

• Thinking of ways to invite—rather than persuade, force, or manipulate—other people to share or use (or even improve) your ideas.

• Locating and questioning assumptions you or others are making about goals or means.

• Imagining in detail how you would behave as an openly cooperative, creative, information-seeking and information-sharing, synergistic sort of person! (Try picking a current troubling situation in your life and working through it in your imagination this way.)

———————————————

○ What are some additional awareness plans that could help you and other people to think synergistically?

INVENTING YOUR OWN

Having sampled a wide range of suggested awareness plans, are you ready to try inventing a few more of your own? This section provides what I think are some helpful tips for doing this. What you will find here as a parting gift are "meta-plans"—procedures to help you devise awareness plans.

However you go about it, though, I think you will more deeply appreciate the central message of this book if you do try your hand at thinking up personally useful awareness plans. That central message, after all, is that you can choose how to experience your world at each moment. The more of yourself you put into this choice, the more you will realize your power to shape your own experience. And while I hope very much that the awareness plans in this book are proving useful and enjoyable for you, inventing your own enables you to tailor new plans to your specific goals, interests, and style.

Ideally, thinking up new awareness plans should be something that is fun and interesting to do. All creative activities should have these qualities. Hence my first bit of advice is to stay loose and playful when using any of the following meta-plans!

Thinking of *Goals*
for New Awareness Plans

Probably the most essential ingredient in cooking up a new awareness plan is to have some destination in mind. So start by asking yourself what you want the plan to accomplish. You can pick a very specific goal, such as inventing a way of thinking about weeds that makes it more fun to pull them out while gardening. Or you can latch onto a vague, general goal like making hobbies more interesting or decreasing anxiety. The important thing is just to get *some* goal in mind.

As a start, see how many goals you can think of right now where awareness plans could be of some service. You might try focusing first on different areas of your life, such as work, family, recreation, distress, and so forth, and then formulating a number of goals within each area. In the area of distress, for instance, possible goals might be easing pain or boredom during an illness, reducing anger or using it constructively, and the like. The more goals and associated awareness plans you think up, the more choice and effectiveness you can inject into your life. (For practice before devising your own awareness plans, you might try brainstorming ways to use various plans from this book to contribute to a few of the goals you think up.)

Using *Questions* to
Generate New Awareness Plans

How many questions can you think of to ask about this scene? Deliberately thinking of questions is an awareness plan that in itself generates new plans almost automatically, since every question can be translated into a particular way of thinking or perceiving. If, for instance, you ask, "Are the kids playing a game?" you can readily translate this into the awareness plan, "Look for cues that indicate whether the kids are playing a game" or perhaps "Guess what sort of game the kids might be playing." Can you translate some of the questions you think of about this scene into new awareness plans that you could use elsewhere as well? Also, how many questions can you quickly generate regarding your current surroundings? What new awareness plans do these questions suggest?

Simply thinking of questions about what is around you is in itself a good way to stir your interest and curiosity. And whenever you set out to *answer* a question, you automatically follow an awareness plan created by the question itself. Notice how your thinking and perception change as you try to answer questions of different types (such as, "Where...?" "Why...?" "How...?" "What if...?").

Using *Metaphors* to
Suggest New Awareness Plans

One of the most effective ways to generate interesting new awareness plans is to interpret things in terms of something else, and then in terms of something else, and so on. You might think of yourself, for instance, as a machine, or a symphony, or a plaything of the gods. Exploring each of these metaphors in depth gives you a different awareness plan about yourself and highlights different aspects of your existence. Or picking formal education as a focus for awareness, you could think of it as an obstacle course, or a stairway (up or down?), or a banquet, and on and on. Again, each of these metaphors gives rise to a new awareness plan for thinking about education.

Right now how many metaphors can you think of for the process of bringing up children? (Some possible examples: gardening; building a house; breaking out of prison; writing a novel.) What new light does each of your metaphors—and the resulting awareness plan—throw on child-rearing for you?

As George Lakoff and Mark Johnson argue in their brilliant little book, *Metaphors We Live By,* metaphorical thinking—understanding something in terms of something else—is a central aspect of human thought. By deliberately trying out new metaphors, drawing new comparisons between apparently different things, we can greatly enliven our thinking and increase our creativity.

Using *Creativity Aids* to Devise New Awareness Plans

This is the big one. Whether you're imagining improvements in things, figuring out action strategies, or creating new awareness plans, using these creativity tips can make an important difference in your fun and success. It is not that creative thinking is ever a rote matter, of course. But you can use these aids, derived from a wide range of theory and research on creativity, to inspire yourself to more original, flexible, and playful thinking. In the end, though, it's naturally up to your own ingenuity, mood, and choice. At the very least, some of these tips may come in handy if you're feeling stuck sometime but really do want to invent a new awareness plan.

As you read over each aid—all are modifications of the list presented in Section V on imagining improvements—take a few minutes to see if you can use it right at that time to generate a new awareness plan or two. The pictures and guiding questions or instructions will point you toward specific purposes, but you can of course choose any goal you like.

1. *Think of things that help you be creative (and re-experience them in your imagination)* — **a good warm-up for any type of creative thinking!**

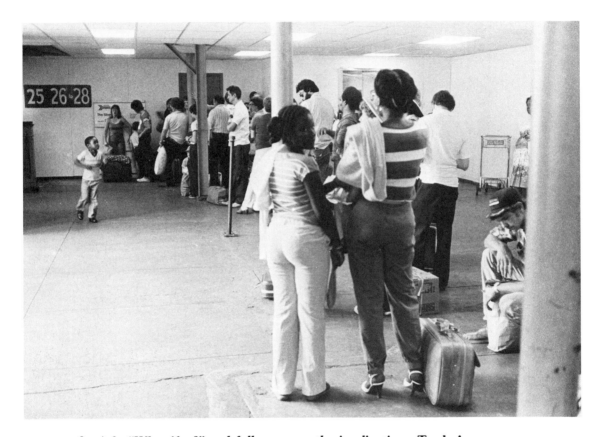

2. *Ask, "What if...?" and follow up on the implications.* To design awareness plans, you might use questions like these: What if I had only one
sense? What if my intelligence were three times what it is (or one-third)?
What if I could read other people's minds or if they could read mine? Now
using these or similar questions, see how many awareness plans you can
devise to make waiting in line more interesting.

3. *Try reversing your goals or ideas.* If you're trying to think up awareness plans to make TV watching more enjoyable, for instance, see what happens if you attempt to devise plans that would make it less enjoyable (and then reverse those awareness plans).

4. *Think of unusual, nutty ways to experience things.* On a car or bike trip, for example, you might think of seeing everything as if you were still and the ground moved, or as if you were on a foreign planet. What other weird awareness plans can you think up to make looking at moving scenery more interesting?

5. *Challenge yourself to invent many alternative awareness plans.* And make each new plan as different as possible from the ones before it. How many different types of awareness plans can you think up right now to make a hobby, such as photography, more enjoyable for you?

6. *Use magical wishes as guides to thinking up creative, but feasible, awareness plans.* **Your magical plan for enjoying your job more, for instance,
might involve experiencing every task as if part of an exciting game or
vacation. What are some awareness plans that might actually introduce
a little of these feelings into your work?**

7. *Think of awareness plans that various types of people (or creatures) might suggest.* For example, what plans that could add interest to your experience of grocery shopping come to mind when you take on each of the following roles: spy, comedian, religious zealot, compulsive collector, speed reader, gardener, fly, package of plastic wrap, stove, fun?

8. *Use all your senses and emotions to suggest new awareness plans.* Can you, say, think of awareness plans linked to smell, to touch, to anger, and to respect that would each add pizzazz to window shopping?

9. *Define the goal for your new awareness plans in different ways.* **If you're looking for plans to perk up your experience of Christmas shopping, for instance, you might define your goal alternatively as (a) helping you think of more interesting presents, (b) alerting yourself to interesting things about the stores or shoppers, or (c) awakening your feelings about any deeper significance of Christmas or gift-giving. What awareness plans can you devise for each of these goals? (P.S. Hey, how about actually giving awareness plans as Christmas presents?!)**

10. *Break the task of devising new awareness plans into subproblems.* **Let's say that for some reason you want to think of humorous ways to experience public monuments. You could break this overall goal into such subgoals as thinking of the types of things you find funny in general; figuring out what might be amusing about specific types of monuments (large ones, small ones, political ones, and so on); and finding ways to apply specific types of humor, such as jokes, puns, exaggerations, and sarcasm.**

11. *Form new mental connections—the wilder, the better.* For instance, starting with anything having to do with railroads or train trips, see if you can
create a few awareness plans to help you enjoy and remember what you
read. (A couple of possible examples: "Thinking of the chapters of a book
as if they were boxcars packed with ideas or images"; "Looking for 'trains
of ideas' running through different things that you read.")

12. *Invent imaginative games that inspire your thinking about new awareness plans.* How, for instance, might you adapt a card game, or tag, or a TV quiz show so that the players would spin off new awareness plans in the course of play? An example would be a form of charades in which a player acts out instructions for a secret awareness plan. As other players try to guess what it is, they would be suggesting new ones themselves!

Grand Finale

To give yourself a grand finale in devising useful awareness plans, first pick a problem or goal of real importance in your life. This can be anything from increasing your enjoyment or ability in some activity (such as your job or studies) to improving some important relationship or even attempting to solve a social problem of widespread concern. The important thing is that this problem or goal really *matter* to you right now. Then see just how much of what you have learned and experienced (and thought up) from the eight sections of this book you can apply to working on your problem or goal.

In keeping with the theme of the current section—creating your own awareness plans—you might concentrate your energy on thinking up *original* ways of experiencing that would help you solve your chosen problem or move toward your goal. But a good warm-up, one that you very likely will find useful, is to go back over the awareness plans in each section and adapt as many of these plans as you can to help you with your problem or goal. For instance, if your goal were to spruce up communication in your marriage, how might you adapt such awareness plans as mentally reversing (Section I), seeing everything as inspiration for a work of art (Section II), or exploring how cultural values shape the things around us (Section IV)? (You might think of such things as reversing roles with your spouse as you argue about something; treating your marriage as a continuing work of art that you and your spouse are creating together; and taking some time to explore together just what your guiding values really are that lead the two of you to talk about whatever you usually do or to spend your time together as you do.)

Although it will take some time and doing to go back through each section to work out special adaptations and applications of the awareness plans there, you should find this creative effort well worth it *if* your goal genuinely matters to you. No kidding, it's a good way to jar your creativity! By working with these highly varied awareness plans to form new uses and connections regarding your problem or goal, you'll be gently forcing yourself to come up with lots of new ideas.

After playing with the plans in this book, go back to the drawing board (if you want still more) and see how many completely new awareness plans you can come up with to help you move toward your goal or deal more effectively with your problem. The meta-plans and creativity aids in the current section might prove especially useful here.

I wish you the best in creatively choosing your experience!

OVERVIEW

SUMMARY LIST OF AWARENESS PLANS & CREATIVITY AIDS

I. Fun and Flexibility

Page

1. Seeing everything around you as *alive* — 14

2. Thinking up past and future *reincarnations* for things around you — 16

3. Dreaming up *alternative meanings* for the things and events around you — 18

4. Interpreting things and events as the *reverse* of what you normally think they are — 20

5. Imagining *new uses* for things around you — 22

6. Viewing the world as if you were an *animal* (or even a *thing*) — 24

II. Aesthetic Awareness

1. Searching your surroundings for everything that strikes you as *beautiful or aesthetically interesting* — 32

2. Looking for scenes in your surroundings that would make the *best photographs* — 34

3. Viewing everyday things as if they were *art exhibits* — 36

4. Experiencing the world as a collection of *abstract forms* — 38

5. Finding special or *unique value* in everything you notice — 40

6. Judging the *degree of beauty* in your surroundings, using many different criteria — 42

7. Regarding everything as a possible *inspiration for a new work of art* — 44

157

III. **Tuning In**

1. Noticing things you *normally wouldn't*   54

2. Searching for *boring* things—and then looking for something interesting about them   56

3. Figuring out what the things and places around you *communicate*   58

4. Thinking about the probable *past and future* of things you notice   60

5. Thinking of something as the *title of a book* and imagining what the book might include   62

IV. **Evaluating**

1. Using *unusual units* of comparison to evaluate people and things around you   70

2. Looking at the world through *different value systems*   72

3. Engaging in an *orgy of evaluation*   74

4. Figuring out the *cultural values* implied by things around you   76

V. **Imagining Improvements**

1. Imagining improvements in *problem spots* around you   82

2. Imagining improvements in already *pleasant things* around you   84

3. Thinking up *actions* that would lead to improvements you imagine   86

Creativity aids for imagining improvements & actions:

  1. Think of everything you can that helps you to be creative.   88

  2. Use "What if…?" questions that challenge your usual assumptions or expectations.   88

  3. Explore reversals of your goals or ideas.   90

4. Deliberately set out to think of unusual, even nutty, things.   90

5. Force yourself to come up with lots of alternative ideas.   92

6. Imagine you have a magic wand.   92

7. Take on different roles as you imagine improvements.   93

8. Use different senses and emotions to suggest new possibilities.   94

9. Define your problem (goal) in many different ways.   94

10. Break the problem into subproblems.   96

11. Form new mental connections.   97

12. Invent imaginative games than can inspire your thinking.   98

VI. Basic Enlightenment

1. Thinking of every moment as an *opportunity*   104

2. Regarding whatever you're doing, thinking, or feeling as if it were your *hobby*   106

3. Thinking of things you can *learn* from whatever you encounter   108

4. For any problematic situation, focusing on what you are doing and especially what *you can do*   110

5. Regarding everything as *perfect* exactly the way it is each moment   112

VII. Synergistic Consciousness

1. Contemplating the total *situation* in which you are enmeshed   120

2. Defining conflicts in terms of *underlying needs* instead of incompatible solutions   122

3. Looking for points in other people's ideas to *build on*   124

4. Thinking of your own and other people's *ideas as gifts* or invitations   126

5. Thinking of *superordinate goals* that would resolve conflicts and excite enthusiasm   128

VIII. Inventing Your Own

1. Thinking of *goals* for new awareness plans   136

2. Using *questions* to generate new awareness plans   138

3. Using *metaphors* to suggest new awareness plans   140

SUPER META-PLAN: Using *creativity aids* to devise new awareness plans:

   1. Think of things that help you be creative (and re-experience them in your imagination).   143

   2. Ask, "What if...?" and follow up on the implications.   144

   3. Try reversing your goals or ideas.   145

   4. Think of unusual, nutty ways to experience things.   146

   5. Challenge yourself to invent many alternative awareness plans.   147

   6. Use magical wishes as guides to thinking up creative, but feasible, awareness plans.   148

   7. Think of awareness plans that various types of people (or creatures) might suggest.   149

   8. Use all your senses and emotions to suggest new awareness plans.   150

   9. Define the goal for your new awareness plans in different ways.   151

  10. Break the task of devising new awareness plans into subproblems.   152

11. Form new mental connections— the wilder,
    the better.   153

12. Invent imaginative games that inspire your
    thinking about new awareness plans.   154

An Invitation

The publisher and I would love to hear from you! We'd welcome your comments on *Playful Perception*, and we're especially eager to find out how you've been applying specific awareness plans or creativity aids—and with what effects. Also, what new awareness plans of your own would you like to share with other readers? Let us know! We'd like to be able to include them in a sequel or a module.

The "modules" are little booklets about applying awareness plans in specific interest areas or professions. Each is being developed in collaboration with professionals in that field. Already in the works are modules for teachers, therapists and counselors, nurses, managers, and people interested in personal financial planning, with more to come. Also under way are workshops on perceptual creativity and plans for a lively, multifaceted parlor game. Your inquiries and suggestions would, of course, be most welcome. We're hoping to form a network of interested people, and we need *you*.

Please write us at:

PLAYFUL PERCEPTION
Waterfront Books
98 Brookes Avenue
Burlington, VT 05401

ABOUT THE AUTHOR: Herbert Leff studied philosophy and psychology at the Universities of South Carolina and North Carolina, and went on to a Ph.D. in social psychology at Harvard. Now a professor at the University of Vermont, he has taught there since 1970 except for a sabbatical year at the University of Hawaii (when the first draft of *Playful Perception* was written). Throughout his career Dr. Leff's central interest has been how psychology can contribute to human happiness—a theme reflected both in this book and in his earlier, more theoretical book, *Experience, Environment, and Human Potentials* (published by Oxford University Press). In addition to teaching psychology and exploring awareness plans, his favorite activities include bicycling, photography, watercolor painting, improvising on the marimba, and playing video games with his son.